Rachel Green's

Chatsworth Cookery Book

A celebration of estate produce
throughout the year

Foreword by the
Dowager Duchess of Devonshire

W9-AYE-393

Rachel Green's
Chatsworth Cookery Book

Editor Victoria Patton
Designer Debbie Lishman
Cover and recipe photography © Michael Powell
Chatsworth photography Jenny Welch
© Chatsworth Settlement Trustees
First published in Great Britain in 2007
by Green Shoots
Beech House
Kingerby
Market Rasen
Lincolnshire LN8 3PF
Green Shoots is a trading name of
Green Shoots Enterprise Ltd
Text copyright © Rachel Green 2007
Design © Green Shoots 2007

Recipe photography reproduction
with kind permission of
www.peas.org
www.britishcarrots.co.uk
www.ukshallots.com
www.british-asparagus.co.uk
www.scholes-ltd.co.uk
www.hillfarmoils.com
www.jackbuckgrowers.co.uk

All rights reserved. No part of this publication may be reproduced, stored in a retrieval system, or transmitted in any form or by any means, electronic, mechanical, photocopying, recording or otherwise, without the prior permission of the copyright owners.

The right of Rachel Green to be identified as the Author of this work has been asserted by her in accordance with the Copyright, Designs and Patents Act 1988

A CIP record for this book is available from the British Library
Printed by GSB, Lincolnshire
ISBN 978-0-9556216-0-4

Contents

When the Chatsworth Farm Shop was set up in 1976 my aim was to sell our produce direct to the people who wanted to eat top quality, locally grown food. It was a novel idea at the time. It is pleasing to note that it has spread and is the accepted principle for food shops throughout the country now.

As a farmer's daughter, it is also Rachel Green's philosophy. We have welcomed her to Chatsworth many times when she has delighted us with her demonstrations and tastings of how to make the best of the best with honest English food.

Now we have her receipts and this book will surely find an enthusiastic audience in the kitchens of our customers and far beyond.

As one who is passionately interested in food, it is my great pleasure to recommend this book.

Debo Devonshire

Dedication

For my son Ollie, my mother Joanna and my late father Derek.

Acknowledgements

To Her Grace, the Dowager Duchess of Devonshire who gave me the wonderful opportunity to be involved with Chatsworth; Lizzie Greaves, Farm Shop Events Manager at Chatsworth who put her job on the line for me! Sara Sweetland who has been unendingly supportive, and all the staff in the Chatsworth farm shop including Paul Neale, the Head Butcher, who have been so welcoming and feel like family; Mary Powell and her team at Tastes of Lincolnshire; Gee Turner, who has assisted me at many Chatsworth demonstrations, her three children, Carla, Fiona and Luke, who have all worked with me, and also Tina Payne; Carol Turner, for her ongoing support above and beyond the call of duty, Jennifer Aspinwall, who has been such a great friend through thick and thin.

To Victoria Patton, for so patiently and meticulously editing the book, Debbie Lishman for her fabulous design; Mike Powell for his outstanding food photography, Jenny Welch at Chatsworth for her wonderful images; Caroline Kenyon, my agent, and Kathleen Codd at Kenyon Communications for their support; Jeni Barrett and Barbara Brandenburger for proof-reading; Peter Doody, Charles and Henry Kenyon and all our Lincolnshire and Derbyshire friends who have supported me at many events; all my family – my brothers Jonathan and Simon - who, as farmers, have taught me so much about food production; and John Churchill for his faith in me.

Rachel Green's
Chatsworth Cookery Book

I feel extremely privileged to be writing this book, just as I have felt privileged to be involved with Chatsworth ever since my first cookery demonstration in the farm shop in 2002. The shop was turned into a theatre in a matter of minutes at the end of the day, with rows of little gilt chairs. The Dowager Duchess of Devonshire, who founded the Chatsworth farm shop and is its inspiration, was sitting in the front row and watching me with her famous amazing blue eyes!

At the heart of good food lie good ingredients. The Chatsworth farm shop was a pioneer of this ethos and continues to be the model of what a good farm shop should be. It has always been a real joy to come and cook with their produce.

The meat produced on the estate is of outstanding quality. It really illustrates the difference that good animal husbandry, along with local abbatoirs and properly hung meat, can make. You will find examples of some of the farmers who supply the shop throughout this book, what they all share is a real love of their animals or produce, and a dedication and skill that is lacking from intensive farming practices. Local, seasonal food is the best way to eat.

This book would never have been possible without the kind permission of the Dowager Duchess, who invited me to Chatsworth five years ago, and to whom I am so grateful. A true visionary, she conceived the idea of the farm shop long before such things became fashionable, and she still takes a great interest in much that goes on there today. What she has created at Chatsworth is very special, and I hope that, through this book, I can share some of it with you.

Spring

to start

Homemade Scotch Eggs with Spicy Shallot, Tomato, Chilli and Ginger Salsa

For the salsa, whisk together the olive oil, cider vinegar and caster sugar. Add the finely chopped shallots and leave for 10 minutes for the shallots to soften slightly in the dressing. Add the tomatoes, chilli and ginger and mix well. Stir through the coriander and season with sea salt and black pepper.

For the Scotch eggs, mix together the sausage meat, sage and Worcestershire sauce and season well with sea salt and black pepper. Divide into four equal portions and shape into flat rounds about 10cm in diameter. Dust the shelled eggs in the seasoned flour and wrap each one in the sausage meat, making sure there are no cracks.

Heat the vegetable oil in a deep saucepan, until it will brown a cube of bread in 50 seconds. Coat the Scotch eggs first in the seasoned flour, then dip in the beaten egg and finally roll in the breadcrumbs, making sure they are well coated.

Carefully lower the Scotch eggs into the hot oil. The sausage meat is raw, so it is essential that the frying should not be too hurried, or they will burn before being cooked through. After 7 - 8 minutes, when they are golden brown, remove them from the oil and drain well. Cool and then cut the Scotch eggs in half lengthways. Serve with the spicy salsa.

For the Scotch eggs

300g Lincolnshire sausage meat
1 tsp sage, finely chopped
½ tsp Worcestershire sauce
4 free range eggs, hard boiled and shelled
4 tbsp plain flour, seasoned
1 egg, beaten
100g fine dry white breadcrumbs
1 litre vegetable oil

For the salsa

8 tbsp olive oil
2 tbsp cider vinegar
2 tsp caster sugar
2 shallots, peeled and finely chopped
2 tomatoes, skinned, deseeded and finely chopped
1 red chilli, deseeded and finely chopped
2cm piece root ginger, peeled and grated
1 small bunch coriander, finely chopped

Makes 4

Carrot and Ginger Soup
with Lemon Herb Cream

Heat the oil in a saucepan, add the onions and carrots and cook for 5 - 10 minutes, stirring from time to time. Do not allow the vegetables to brown.

Add the garlic, ginger and curry powder to the pan and cook for a further minute. Add the stock and lemon zest, bring to the boil and simmer for 25 - 30 minutes, or until the carrots are tender. Liquidise the soup until smooth, taste and season with sea salt and black pepper.

To make the lemon herb cream, mix together the crème fraiche, lemon zest and herbs. Reheat the soup and spoon a dollop of the lemon herb cream into the middle of each bowl. Serve with crusty wholemeal bread.

2 tbsp olive oil
2 onions,
peeled and chopped
600g carrots,
peeled and chopped
1 clove garlic,
peeled and crushed
1 tsp ground ginger
1 tsp medium curry powder
900ml good stock,
chicken or vegetable
1 lemon, zested

For the lemon herb cream
200g crème fraiche
1 lemon, zested
1 tbsp parsley,
finely chopped
1 tbsp chives,
finely chopped

Serves 4

Lancashire Cheese Beignets
with Redcurrant Confit

85g plain flour
Pinch salt
150ml water
55g butter, diced
2 eggs, beaten
100g Lancashire cheese
1 litre vegetable oil

For the redcurrant confit
110g redcurrants
1 tbsp caster sugar
1 tbsp water
55g redcurrant jelly
Juice ½ lemon

Serves 4

Sift the flour and salt together into a bowl. Place the water and butter in a small saucepan over a medium heat. Allow the butter to melt, then bring to a rolling boil. Remove from the heat and stir in the sifted flour. Beat the mixture for about a minute until it is smooth and leaving the sides of the pan. Leave to cool slightly, then add the beaten egg gradually, beating well after each addition, until the mixture is smooth and shiny. Crumble the Lancashire cheese and add to the mixture, along with some freshly ground black pepper. Chill until ready to use.

For the redcurrant confit, place the redcurrants in a pan with the caster sugar and water and cook very gently until they have softened. Add the redcurrant jelly and lemon juice and continue to cook over a gentle heat until most of the liquid has evaporated and the confit is thick, syrupy and glossy.

Heat the vegetable oil in a deep saucepan and fry spoonfuls of the beignet mixture for 2 - 3 minutes, until puffed up and golden brown. Drain well on paper towel and serve with the warm redcurrant confit.

At Chatsworth farm shop we're passionate about British cheeses. Expert cheese maker Bob Kitching makes all his cheeses by hand and has won many awards for his produce.

Bob Kitching, Leagram Organic Dairy, Lancashire.

Celeriac and Mushroom Hash
with Soft Poached Eggs and Smoked Salmon

Place the celeriac, bay leaf and milk in a saucepan and bring to the boil. Simmer for 15 - 20 minutes, until the celeriac is tender. Drain and mash roughly.

Meanwhile, heat the butter and olive oil in a frying pan and add the bacon. Cook over a medium heat until golden and then add the onion and garlic. Lower the heat and cook for 8 - 10 minutes, until the onion is soft and translucent. Add the mushrooms and thyme and cook for a further 10 minutes, stirring from time to time. Add this mixture to the celeriac mash and mix thoroughly. Season well with sea salt and black pepper.

Spoon this mixture back into the frying pan and press down well. Cook over a medium heat, stirring from time to time to break the hash up, until it is golden brown throughout.

While the hash is cooking, bring a pan of water to the boil, then turn down to a slow simmer. Crack each egg into a ramekin or cup and slip gently into the simmering water. Poach for 3 minutes, remove and drain well.

Serve the celeriac and mushroom hash with the poached eggs and smoked salmon and garnish with the chopped chives.

350g celeriac, peeled and diced
1 bay leaf
600ml milk
55g butter
1 tbsp olive oil
110g smoked streaky bacon, sliced
1 onion, peeled and finely chopped
2 cloves garlic, peeled and crushed
110g button mushrooms, sliced
1 tbsp thyme, finely chopped
4 eggs
200g smoked salmon, sliced
1 tbsp chives, finely chopped, to garnish

Serves 4

Asparagus with Warm Potato Pancakes,
Bacon and Hollandaise

First make the potato pancakes. Mix together the mashed potato, egg and flour until smooth. Season well and fold in the double cream, the mixture should resemble thick porridge. Heat the butter and oil in a large frying pan and fry the batter, a couple of tablespoons at a time, to make thick pancakes. Cook over a medium heat until golden brown, then turn and cook for a further 1 - 2 minutes, until the pancakes are cooked through and firm to the touch. Keep warm in a low oven.

For the hollandaise, place the white wine vinegar in a small pan with the bay leaf and peppercorns, boil until reduced to 1 tablespoon and leave to cool. Melt the butter. Place the egg yolks and cooled vinegar reduction in the bowl of a food processor. With the motor running, drizzle in the hot melted butter very slowly until an emulsion forms. You can then add the butter a little more quickly. Season with the lemon juice as you go, this will also help prevent the sauce from becoming too thick. If it looks like curdling, simply add a little cold water and it will come back together. Once all the butter has been incorporated, season the hollandaise and keep warm in a water bath.

Bring a large pan of water to the boil and cook the asparagus for 6 - 7 minutes until tender to the point of a knife. Grill or pan fry the bacon until crisp. Serve the potato pancakes with the asparagus, crisp bacon and hollandaise sauce.

2 bundles British asparagus
8 rashers thinly-cut smoked streaky bacon

For the potato pancakes
500g cold mashed potato
1 egg, beaten
60g plain flour
100ml double cream
25g butter
1 tbsp vegetable oil

For the hollandaise
2 egg yolks
110g unsalted butter
3 tbsp white wine vinegar
1 bay leaf
6 black peppercorns
1 tbsp lemon juice

Serves 4

Spring

Spring

main courses

Salmon Fish Cakes
with Sorrel Sauce

Place the salmon fillet on a large double thickness of tin foil. Cut the lemon in half, reserve one half for the sorrel sauce and cut the other half into slices. Place the lemon slices on top of the salmon with the bay leaf and season with sea salt and black pepper. Fold the foil over the top and seal the edges together. Place the foil parcel on a baking sheet and bake in the preheated oven for 10 minutes, until the salmon is just cooked. Remove from the oven and leave to cool.

Place the mashed potato in a bowl and mix in the anchovy essence, mustard, mayonnaise and parsley. Season to taste and mix until well combined. Flake in the salmon and fold through gently. Shape the mixture into 4 fishcakes and chill for 2 hours.

Dust the fishcakes in the seasoned flour. Melt the butter with the oil in a frying pan and fry the fishcakes until golden brown on each side. Turn down the heat and cook for a further 10 minutes, or until the fishcakes are cooked through. Alternatively, they can be finished off in the oven.

Meanwhile, make the sorrel sauce. Place the fish stock, vermouth and white wine in a saucepan, bring to the boil and reduce to 150ml. Add the double cream and simmer until the sauce is thick enough to coat the back of a spoon. Whisk in the butter, add a little lemon juice, season and stir in the sorrel. Serve the fishcakes accompanied by the sorrel sauce, with lemon wedges on the side.

600g salmon fillet
1 lemon
1 bay leaf
500g potato,
cooked, mashed and cooled
1 tsp anchovy essence
1 tsp English mustard
1 tbsp mayonnaise
2 tbsp parsley,
finely chopped
3 tbsp plain flour, seasoned
30g butter
1 tbsp oil
Lemon wedges, to serve

For the sorrel sauce
500ml fish stock
50ml vermouth
100ml dry white wine
125ml double cream
50g unsalted butter
25g young sorrel leaves,
washed and finely shredded

Serves 4

Preheat the oven to
180°C/350°F/Gas Mark 4

Spring

Pea, Spring Onion and Rocket Risotto

Bring half the stock to the boil with half the peas and simmer for 5 minutes. Blend well in a food processor or with a hand held blender. Pour back into the pan and add the remaining stock.

Heat half the butter with the oil in a large, heavy based pan. Add the garlic and spring onions and cook gently for 2 minutes. Add the rice, stir well so that it is coated with the buttery juices and cook for 2 minutes.

Add enough pea stock to cover the rice and stir continually until it is absorbed. Continue to cook, stirring and adding more stock as necessary, until the rice is al dente. This will take 15 - 20 minutes.

Stir in the remaining peas with the last addition of stock and cook for a further five minutes. Add the rocket and stir until the leaves have wilted. Remove from the heat, stir in the remaining butter, parmesan and parsley and season to taste.

Serve the risotto in warm bowls with extra parmesan on top.

1.2 litres vegetable stock
500g frozen peas
50g butter
2 tbsp olive oil
2 cloves garlic,
peeled and crushed
10 spring onions,
topped, tailed and sliced
300g Arborio risotto rice
100g rocket, washed
50g freshly grated
Parmesan,
plus extra to serve
1 tbsp flat leaved parsley,
finely chopped

Serves 4

Pan-Fried Danebridge River Trout
with Grapefruit and Avocado Salsa

8 fillets brown river trout, skin on
1 tbsp olive oil
30g butter

For the salsa
1 pink grapefruit
1 mango,
peeled, stoned and diced
1 avocado,
peeled, stoned and diced
1 red chilli, deseeded and finely chopped
6 spring onions, finely sliced
1 tbsp extra virgin olive oil
1 lime, juiced

Serves 4

First make the salsa. Peel and segment the grapefruit, catching any juice as you do so. Mix together with the mango, avocado, chilli and spring onions and dress with the extra virgin olive oil and lime juice. Season with sea salt and black pepper and leave to infuse for 30 minutes so that the flavours can develop.

Heat the butter with the oil in a frying pan. Season the trout fillets and pan fry, skin side down, over a high heat for 1 minute, until the skin is crisp and golden. Turn the fillets over, lower the heat and cook for a further minute until the fish is just cooked through.

Serve with the grapefruit and avocado salsa.

The fish at Danebridge Trout bask in ponds fed by the River Dane as it runs off the back of the Roaches and the moors of the Goyt Valley

Lorne Chadwick, Danebridge Trout, Macclesfield.

Chicken with Chilli, Feta and Streaky Bacon with Tomato and Onion Dressing

Lay the chicken breasts upside down on a chopping board. Using a sharp knife, make an incision under the false fillet and carefully open it out to make a pocket. Roughly crumble the feta cheese and use to stuff the chicken breasts. Smooth the false fillet back over the top of the feta and wrap two pieces of streaky bacon around each chicken breast. Secure with cocktail sticks and place in a roasting tin. Drizzle with the olive oil and roast in the preheated oven for 25 minutes.

Meanwhile, make the tomato and onion dressing. Roughly chop the tomatoes and place in a bowl. Add the onion, chilli, coriander, lime juice and olive oil, season and leave for 20 minutes to allow the flavours to develop.

To serve, place a handful of rocket on each plate, place the breast of chicken on top and drizzle with the dressing. Garnish with lime wedges.

4 breasts chicken, skinned
200g feta cheese
8 rashers rindless streaky bacon
2 tbsp olive oil
100g rocket leaves
Lime wedges to garnish

For the tomato and onion dressing
4 large ripe tomatoes, blanched and peeled
1 red onion, peeled and finely chopped
1 red chilli, deseeded and finely chopped
1 bunch coriander, washed, dried and roughly chopped
2 limes, juiced
1 tbsp olive oil

Serves 4

Preheat the oven to 180°C/350°F/Gas Mark 4

Spring

Roasted Duck Breast
with Wilted Spinach and Braised Rhubarb

4 duck breasts
1 tbsp runny honey
1 orange, zested and juiced

For the braised rhubarb
500g rhubarb, trimmed and cut into 5cm lengths
2cm fresh root ginger, peeled and finely diced
1 tbsp soft brown sugar
50ml Marsala
20g unsalted butter

For the wilted spinach
750g young spinach leaves, washed
30g unsalted butter
1 tbsp rapeseed oil
1 clove garlic, crushed
Grating of nutmeg

Serves 4

Preheat the oven to
200°C/400°F/Gas Mark 6

For the braised rhubarb, place the trimmed rhubarb in a saucepan with the orange zest, ginger, brown sugar and Marsala. Cover and cook on a gentle heat for 10 - 15 minutes, until the rhubarb is tender. Lift the rhubarb out with a slotted spoon and place in a bowl. Bring the liquid to the boil and reduce to a syrup. Pour over the rhubarb and keep warm.

Trim the duck breasts of any excess fat and criss-cross the skin with a sharp knife, making sure that you score only the skin and fat and not the flesh. Rub some salt into the skin. Place the duck breasts in a heavy-based frying pan and cook over a medium heat so that the fat renders down and the skin becomes brown and crisp. Remove the duck breasts from the pan and place in a roasting tin. Mix together the honey and orange juice and brush this mixture over the duck breasts. Roast in the preheated oven for 8 - 10 minutes, depending on the size of the duck breasts.

Heat the butter and rapeseed oil in a large saucepan. Add the spinach leaves, cover and cook over a medium heat for 1 minute until they are starting to wilt. Add the garlic and a grating of nutmeg to the pan and season with sea salt and black pepper and toss this into the spinach. Cook for a further minute or two, until the spinach is wilted.

Remove the duck breasts from the oven and leave to rest for a few minutes before carving into thick slices. Serve with the wilted spinach and braised rhubarb.

main courses

Lamb's Liver with Pea Purée,
Pancetta and Sage Butter

First make the pea purée. Melt the butter in a saucepan, add the onion, cover and cook over a gentle heat for 10 minutes until softened and translucent. Stir in the peas, coat with the buttery juices, then add the stock and bring to the boil. Simmer for 5 minutes, then add the caster sugar, nutmeg and cream and season well with sea salt and black pepper. Purée with a hand blender and keep warm.

Dust the lamb's liver in the seasoned flour. Melt the butter with the oil in a large frying pan and pan fry the liver for 2 - 3 minutes on each side. In a separate pan, fry the pancetta until golden brown and crispy, then add the sage and unsalted butter.

Serve the liver with the pea purée, with the pancetta and sage butter drizzled over the top.

**750g lamb's liver,
cut into thick slices
2 tbsp plain flour, seasoned
20g butter
1 tbsp olive oil**

**For the pancetta and
sage butter**

**150g pancetta,
cut into lardons
Small bunch sage,
finely chopped
30g unsalted butter**

For the pea purée

**30g butter
1 onion, peeled and finely
chopped
500g frozen peas
50ml vegetable stock
½ tsp caster sugar
Grating of nutmeg
2 tbsp double cream**

Serves 4

Mussel and Shallot Broth

First check through the mussels, discarding any that are cracked or do not close when tapped sharply. Remove any 'beards' and rinse under cold running water.

In a large, deep pan with a lid, melt the butter with the olive oil. Add the shallots, cover and cook gently for 10 minutes, until softened and translucent. Add the garlic and cook for a further 2 minutes. Pour in the white wine, bring to the boil and add the mussels. Cover and cook for 4 minutes.

Tip the mussels into a colander set over a bowl to catch the liquid. Return the liquid to the pan, bring to the boil and reduce slightly. Add the double cream, season and boil for 2 minutes. Meanwhile, transfer the mussels to a large serving dish, discarding any that have not opened during the cooking process. Add the parsley and chives to the sauce and pour over the mussels. Serve with plenty of warm, crusty bread.

1 kg mussels, scrubbed
30g butter
1 tbsp olive oil
4 shallots,
peeled and finely chopped
2 cloves garlic,
peeled and crushed
300ml white wine
200ml double cream
2 tbsp parsley,
finely chopped
1 tbsp chives,
finely chopped

Serves 4

Lamb, Carrot and Rosemary Cobbler

600g lamb leg or
shoulder, diced
3 tbsp plain flour, seasoned
2 tbsp olive oil
4 carrots,
peeled and thickly sliced
1 onion
1 leek,
trimmed and thickly sliced
2 cloves garlic, crushed
1 tsp rosemary,
finely chopped
1 bay leaf
1 tbsp redcurrant jelly
850ml lamb or
vegetable stock

For the cobbler
225g self-raising flour
½ tsp salt
50g butter, diced and chilled
120ml milk
2 eggs
1 tsp dried rosemary
50g Cheddar cheese, grated
Beaten egg, to glaze

Serves 4

Preheat the oven to
180°C/350°F/Gas Mark 4

Toss the lamb in the seasoned flour. Heat the oil in a large casserole. Brown the meat in batches, remove and set aside. Add the carrot, onion and leek and cook, stirring from time to time, for 5 - 10 minutes, until the vegetables are lightly browned and starting to soften. Add the garlic and cook for a further minute. Add the rosemary, bay leaf and redcurrant jelly and blend in the stock. Season, cover and cook in the preheated oven for 1 hour, until the lamb is almost tender.

Turn the oven up to 220°C/425°F/Gas Mark 7. Sift the flour with the salt into a large bowl. Rub in the chilled butter until the mixture resembles breadcrumbs. Stir in the rosemary and grated cheese. Beat the eggs in a jug and add the milk. Make a well in the centre of the mixture and add the liquid. Bring together with a knife to form a soft dough and knead lightly, the mixture will be sticky. Roll out on a floured surface to 3cm thick and cut into rounds with a floured cutter.

Put the scones directly on top of the casserole and brush with beaten egg for a golden crust. Cook in the preheated oven for 15 - 20 minutes, until the cobbler is well risen and golden brown.

main courses

Tagine of Derbyshire Poussins
with Preserved Lemons and Olives

Soak the saffron in the boiling water and leave to infuse. Season the poussins inside and out. Melt half the butter with the oil in a casserole dish and brown the poussins on all sides. Remove from the pan and add the remaining butter and oil. Add the shallots and cook for 5 minutes until softened. Add the garlic, ginger and harissa and cook for a further 2 minutes.

Add the stock and infused saffron tea. Bring to the boil, turn down to a simmer and return the poussins to the pan. Cover with a tight-fitting lid and cook slowly for 30 minutes, turning the poussins over in the sauce several times.

Cut the preserved lemons into thick slices and rinse well to remove any salt. Add to the pan with the olives, coriander and parsley. Cook for a further 15 minutes, adjust the seasoning and serve with couscous.

4 whole poussins
2 tbsp olive oil
30g butter
4 shallots,
peeled and finely chopped
4 cloves garlic,
peeled and crushed
2 tsp ground ginger
2 tsp hot harissa paste
500ml chicken stock
½ tsp saffron
100ml boiling water
2 preserved lemons
125g green, stoned olives
1 bunch coriander,
finely chopped
3 tbsp flat leaved parsley,
finely chopped

Serves 4

Rack of Lamb
with Mint Aiöli and Sweet Potato Chips

Heat 1 tablespoon of oil in a large frying pan or griddle and sear the lamb well on all sides. Transfer to a roasting tin and roast in the preheated oven for 20 minutes.

Place the sweet potato chips in a large roasting tin and drizzle with the remaining 2 tablespoons of oil. Season well with sea salt and black pepper and roast in the preheated oven for 15 - 20 minutes, until golden and cooked through.

For the aiöli, mix the egg yolks, crushed garlic and mustard in the bowl of a food processor. With the motor running, slowly drizzle in the oil, a few drops at a time until the mixture has started to emulsify and then in a slow but steady stream. If the aioli becomes too thick at any stage or looks like it is in danger of curdling then add a few drops of lemon juice. Once all the oil has been incorporated, add the mayonnaise, stir through the mint and season with sea salt, black pepper and lemon juice to taste.

Remove the lamb from the oven and allow to rest for 5 minutes, before carving into cutlets and serving with the sweet potato chips and mint aiöli.

2 racks of lamb
3 tbsp Hillfarm rapeseed oil
1 kg sweet potatoes,
peeled and cut into chips

For the aioli
2 egg yolks
3 cloves garlic,
peeled and crushed
1 tsp Dijon mustard
200ml Hillfarm rapeseed oil
1 tbsp lemon juice
2 tbsp mint, finely chopped
1 tbsp mayonnaise

Serves 4

Preheat the oven to
200°C/400°F/Gas Mark 6

Spring

Spring

puddings

Chocolate-Crusted Lemon Tart

First make the pastry. Sift together the flour, cocoa, salt and icing sugar. Rub in the cold butter using a food processor or your fingertips until the mixture resembles fine breadcrumbs. Mix the egg yolk with the cold water and add to the mixture to bring together. Shape the pastry into a flat disc and chill in the fridge for half an hour. Roll out the pastry and use to line a 23cm loose-bottomed tart tin. Prick the base with a fork and chill for half an hour or until the pastry is solid.

Line the pastry case with a circle of greaseproof paper, fill with baking beans and bake blind for 15 minutes. Remove the beans and bake for a further 2 - 3 minutes until the pastry is dry and biscuity. While the pastry is still hot, scatter the grated chocolate evenly over the base and leave to cool. Reduce the oven temperature to 170°C/350°F/Gas Mark 3.

To make the filling, zest and juice the lemons into a mixing bowl. Add the sugar and whisk until it has dissolved. Add the eggs and cream and whisk until smooth. Pour the filling into the cooled pastry case and return it to the oven. Bake for 30 - 35 minutes until just set. Remove from the oven and leave on a wire rack to cool completely before removing from the tin.

Dust with icing sugar before serving.

For the pastry
175g plain flour
25g cocoa
Pinch of salt
25g icing sugar
125g unsalted butter, chilled and diced
1 large egg yolk
2 tablespoons cold water

For the filling
75g dark chocolate (70% cocoa solids)
3 juicy unwaxed lemons
150g caster sugar
4 large eggs
150ml double cream
Icing sugar to serve

Serves 6

Preheat the oven to 200°C/400°F/Gas Mark 6

Spring

Rhubarb and Stem Ginger Fool

Cut the rhubarb into even sized lengths and place in an ovenproof dish with the sugar and orange juice. Cover tightly with foil and cook in the preheated oven for 30 minutes. Sprinkle over the ginger and leave to cool.

Place the milk in a saucepan with the vanilla pod and bring to the boil. Remove the vanilla pod and scrape the seeds into the milk. Whisk together the egg yolks and caster sugar and pour on the hot milk, whisking all the time. Return the mixture to the pan and cook over a gentle heat until it thickens enough to coat the back of a spoon. Strain immediately into a bowl and leave to cool. Whip the cream into soft peaks and fold lightly into the custard, to create a marbled effect.

Assemble the pudding in glasses. Layer the rhubarb and ginger alternately with the creamy custard mixture, finishing with some rhubarb on the top. Chill until ready to serve.

900g young, pink rhubarb
200g granulated sugar
1 orange, juiced
1 tbsp stem ginger,
finely chopped
250ml full fat milk
1 vanilla pod, halved
55g caster sugar
5 large egg yolks
290ml double cream

Serves 6

Preheat the oven to
150°C/300°F/Gas Mark 2

Hot Chatsworth Chocolate Fondant Puddings

**350g dark chocolate
(70% cocoa solids)
50g unsalted butter,
softened
150g caster sugar
4 large eggs
1 tsp vanilla essence
50g plain flour**

Serves 6

Preheat the oven to
200°C/400°F/Gas Mark 6

Line 6 dariole moulds with a circle of baking parchment in the base.

Bring a pan of water to the boil, then remove from the heat. Break up the chocolate into a glass bowl and set this over the pan of water. Allow to melt slowly, stirring from time to time.

In a separate bowl, cream together the softened butter with the caster sugar until pale. Add the eggs, one at a time, beating well after each addition and then the vanilla essence. Fold in the flour and, lastly, the warm melted chocolate.

Divide the mixture between the dariole moulds and place on a baking sheet in the preheated oven. The puddings can be refrigerated at this stage and cooked from the fridge at a later stage. Cook for 10 - 12 minutes (10 if cooking straight away, 12 if cooking from the fridge). The puddings should be springy to the touch, but still molten in the centre. Turn out onto plates and serve with cream, crème fraiche or icecream.

Tony Robb, Head Baker at Chatsworth farm shop, has been perfecting his art for more than 30 years. His son also works in the bakery, bringing together the skills of two generations

Tony Robb,
Chatsworth farm shop bakery.

Banana and Cardamom Tarte Tatin

Melt the butter in a 20cm ovenproof frying pan. Add the caster sugar and cook over a medium heat. Crush the cardamom pods, remove the seeds and add to the pan. Increase the heat and cook to a caramel, swirling the pan to ensure that it colours evenly. Remove from the heat.

Peel the bananas, slice thickly and toss in a little lemon juice. Add the bananas to the pan, cut side down, packing them in tightly. Roll out the puff pastry to a round just larger than the diameter of the pan. Lay the pastry carefully over the top of the bananas and tuck in the edges. Place the pan on a baking sheet and cook in the preheated oven for 25 minutes, until the pastry has risen and is golden brown.

Remove from the oven and leave to cool for 1 minute, so that the caramel is not too runny. Then invert a serving plate over the top of the pan and carefully turn out the tarte tatin. Dust with icing sugar and serve with clotted cream or vanilla icecream.

110g unsalted butter
110g caster sugar
10 cardamom pods
6 large bananas
1 lemon, juiced
500g all butter puff pastry
Icing sugar to serve

Serves 6 - 8

Preheat the oven to
200°C/400°F/Gas Mark 6

Spring

Cherry Clafoutis

450g cherries, stoned
100ml milk
150ml double cream
1 vanilla pod, split in half
4 eggs
140g caster sugar
30g plain flour
Butter and caster sugar for
greasing and sprinkling

Serves 6 - 8

Preheat the oven to
200°C/400°F/Gas Mark 6.

Butter an ovenproof dish and sprinkle with caster sugar. Put the milk, cream and vanilla pod in a small saucepan. Bring to the boil then turn off the heat and leave to infuse.

Place the eggs and sugar in a large bowl and whisk until pale. Add the flour and whisk again until smooth. Remove the vanilla pod and scrape the seeds into the infused milk and cream. Pour this gradually into the egg mixture and stir until well combined. Place the cherries in the buttered dish and pour over the batter.

Bake in the pre-heated oven for 25 minutes until risen and golden brown. Allow to cool slightly, dust with icing sugar and serve with cream or crème fraiche.

puddings

Spring

Summer

to start

Crab and Prawn Tian
with Celeriac Remoulade and a Herb Dressing

For the herb dressing, whisk all the ingredients together and season with sea salt and black pepper.

For the celeriac remoulade, grate the celeriac on the coarse attachment of the food processor, or cut into julienne strips. Place in a bowl and mix in the remaining ingredients. Season with sea salt and black pepper.

Next prepare the fish. In one bowl, mix together the crab meat with 1 tablespoon of the dressing and a few drops of Tabasco. In another bowl, mix the prawns with the mayonnaise and spring onions. Lightly season both with sea salt and black pepper.

To assemble, use a plain cutter, 7 - 8cm in diameter. Place in the middle of a plate and spoon in a quarter of the crab followed by a quarter of the prawns, pressing down well. Remove the cutter and repeat this process on the other three plates. Place a spoonful of remoulade next to each tian and drizzle each plate with some herb dressing. Grind over some black pepper and serve immediately.

180g fresh white crab meat
180g cooked peeled prawns,
roughly chopped
1 tbsp mayonnaise
2 spring onions,
finely sliced
Few drops Tabasco

For the celeriac remoulade
1 medium celeriac, peeled
200ml mayonnaise
2 tbsp Dijon mustard
1 tbsp wholegrain mustard
1 tbsp horseradish
1 lemon, juiced
1 tbsp chives,
finely chopped

For the herb dressing
5 tbsp olive oil
½ lemon, juiced
1 tbsp white wine vinegar
1 tbsp sherry vinegar
½ tsp dry mustard
1 tbsp parsley,
finely chopped
1 tbsp chives,
finely chopped

Serves 4

Summer

Grilled Halloumi
with Broad Bean, Pea and Rocket Salad

First make the dressing. Whisk together the oil, lemon juice, caster sugar and garlic. Stir in the mint and chilli, season and set aside.

Cook the broad beans in a pan of lightly salted boiling water for 3 - 4 minutes. Drain and refresh under cold running water. Peel off the grey outer skins. Bring another pan of water to the boil, add the peas and return to the boil. Drain and refresh under cold running water. Place the cooked beans and peas in a large bowl. Add the spring onions and rocket leaves, pour in the dressing, season and toss the salad together.

Preheat the grill to high. Place the halloumi on a greased baking sheet and grill for 2 minutes on each side, until golden and bubbling. Divide the salad between four plates and top each plate with three slices of halloumi. Grind over some black pepper and serve.

2 x 250g packets Halloumi cheese, each cut into 6 slices
150g broad beans, shelled
200g frozen peas
4 spring onions, finely sliced
2 large handfuls rocket

For the dressing
5 tbsp extra virgin olive oil
1 lemon, juiced
1 tsp caster sugar
1 clove garlic, peeled and crushed
1 tbsp mint, finely chopped
1 red chilli, deseeded and finely chopped

Serves 4

Summer

Tomato, Ricotta and Watercress Tart

with a Tomato Vinaigrette

For the pastry
200g plain flour
Pinch of salt
100g unsalted butter,
diced and chilled
1 egg yolk mixed with
2 tbsp cold water

For the filling
2 bunches watercress
2 tomatoes,
peeled and sliced
Small bunch basil leaves,
roughly torn
150g ricotta cheese
3 egg yolks
100ml double cream
100ml crème fraiche

For the tomato vinaigrette
6 tbsp extra virgin olive oil
1 tbsp lemon juice
1 tbsp white wine vinegar
1 clove garlic,
peeled and crushed
4 tomatoes, peeled,
deseeded and finely
chopped
1 tbsp chives,
finely chopped
1 tbsp basil,
finely chopped
1 tbsp parsley,
finely chopped

Serves 6 - 8

Preheat the oven to
200°C/400°F/Gas Mark 6

First make the pastry. Sift the flour with the salt into the bowl of a food processor. Add the diced, chilled butter and pulse until the mixture resembles fine breadcrumbs. Tip into a large bowl and add the egg yolk and water mixture. Stir until the mixture comes together. Roll out the pastry and use to line a 20cm loose bottomed flan tin. Chill for 30 minutes, or until the pastry is solid.

Line the pastry case with a circle of greaseproof paper, fill with baking beans and bake blind for 15 minutes. Remove the beans and bake for a further 2 - 3 minutes until the pastry is dry and biscuity. Turn the oven down to 170°C/325°F/Gas Mark 3.

Bring a pan of water to the boil, add the watercress, cook for 30 seconds, then drain and refresh under cold running water. Squeeze dry and roughly chop. Arrange the watercress in the bottom of the pastry case, followed by the sliced tomatoes. Scatter over the torn basil leaves and crumble over the ricotta cheese. Mix together the egg yolks, cream and crème fraiche and season well. Pour into the pastry case and bake for 30 - 40 minutes, until the tart is set and golden on top.

Meanwhile, make the tomato vinaigrette. Whisk together the extra virgin olive oil, lemon juice, white wine vinegar and crushed garlic. Add the chopped tomatoes and herbs and season. Serve the tart warm, accompanied by the tomato vinaigrette.

to start

Honeyed Fig and Poacher Cheese Salad

Trim the stems off the figs and cut a cross in the top of each one. Gently press the base of each fig, so that it opens up like a flower. Mix together the honey, lemon juice and olive oil until the honey has dissolved and drizzle over the figs. Season with sea salt and black pepper and set aside to marinade for 20 minutes.

Bring a large pan of salted water to the boil and add the green beans. Blanch for 2 - 3 minutes, drain and refresh under cold running water. Using a potato peeler, shave off slices of the Lincolnshire Poacher cheese. Rinse the salad leaves and drain well. Arrange in a salad bowl or on a large platter with the green beans and sliced tomatoes. Scatter over the toasted almonds and cheese and top with the marinaded figs. Spoon over the remaining marinade as a dressing and serve.

4 figs
1 tbsp runny honey
1 lemon, juiced
4 tbsp extra virgin olive oil
200g green beans, topped
2 heads chicory, sliced
2 large handfuls rocket
1 bunch watercress
4 large tomatoes, sliced
150g Lincolnshire Poacher cheese
50g blanched almonds, toasted

Serves 4

Barbecued Asparagus
with Rocket, Goat's Cheese and Pinenuts

Toss the asparagus in the oil, making sure it is well coated and season with sea salt and black pepper. Cook the asparagus on the grill rack of the barbecue for 2 - 3 minutes each side, until it is lightly charred and cooked through.

To make the dressing, mix all the ingredients together and whisk well. Season to taste.

Divide the rocket between four plates. Top with the barbecued asparagus, crumble over the goats cheese, sprinkle with the toasted pine nuts and drizzle over the dressing. Serve immediately with warm, crusty bread.

2 bundles British asparagus
2 tbsp olive or rapeseed oil
100g rocket, washed
150g goat's cheese
55g pine nuts, toasted

For the dressing
3 tbsp olive or rapeseed oil
1 tbsp lemon juice
2 tsp grainy mustard
1tbsp runny honey

Serves 4

Summer

Summer

main courses

Chatsworth Gammon with Broad Bean Purée and Parsley Cream Sauce

Place the cream, milk, bay leaf, onion, peppercorns, mace and parsley stalks in a saucepan and bring to the boil. Turn off the heat and leave to infuse for half an hour, then strain. Melt the butter, add the flour and cook over a medium heat for 1 minute. Remove from the heat and whisk in half the infused creamy milk. Return to the heat, stirring all the time as the sauce thickens. Gradually add the rest of the liquid and simmer until the sauce has thickened and is smooth and glossy. Season with sea salt and black pepper.

Next prepare the broad bean purée. Melt the butter in a saucepan and add the shallots. Cover and cook over a gentle heat for 5 - 10 minutes, until the shallots have softened and are translucent. Add the garlic and cook for a further minute. Add the broad beans and cream and cook for a further 2 - 3 minutes. Season, purée and keep warm.

For the gammon, melt the butter with the oil in a heavy based frying pan. Remove any rind from the gammon steaks and snip the fat at regular intervals with a pair of scissors so that the meat remains flat and does not curl up whilst cooking. Season the meat and cook in the hot pan for 2 - 3 minutes on each side, depending on the thickness of the steaks.

Reheat the cream sauce and add the parsley. Serve the gammon on the broad bean purée, with the parsley cream sauce on the side.

4 gammon steaks
25g butter
1tbsp oil

For the broad bean purée
50g butter
2 shallots,
peeled and finely diced
1 clove garlic,
peeled and crushed
500g Shelled broad beans,
blanched and skinned
2 tbsp double cream

For the parsley cream sauce
125ml double cream
300ml full fat milk
1 bay leaf
1 onion, peeled and sliced
A pinch of mace
8 black peppercorns
50g butter
25g plain flour
4 tbsp parsley, finely
chopped (reserve the stalks)

Serves 4

Summer

Chargrilled Tuna
with Tomato, Coriander and Lime Salsa

First make the salsa. Quarter and deseed the tomatoes, then chop into even sized dice. Mix with the red onion and coriander, then dress with the oil and lime juice. Season well with sea salt and black pepper and set aside. The salsa is improved by being made an hour or so in advance, to allow the flavours to develop.

Heat a ridged griddle pan until smoking hot. Brush the tuna steaks with the oil and season with sea salt and black pepper. Sear the tuna for a minute on each side for rare, or a minute and a half for medium. Serve the tuna steaks with the salsa and garnish with lime wedges.

**4 x 180g thick cut
tuna steaks
1 tbsp Hillfarm rapeseed oil**

For the salsa
**4 ripe tomatoes
1 red onion, peeled and
finely chopped
Small bunch coriander,
roughly chopped
4 tbsp Hillfarm rapeseed oil
1 lime, juiced
Lime wedges, to garnish**

Serves 4

Summer

Lamb with Courgettes,
Pink Grapefruit and Feta Cheese

4 x 180g lamb fillets
(from best end)
1 tbsp oil
2 courgettes, thickly sliced
2 pink grapefruit
4 spring onions,
halved and cut into strips
2 tbsp fresh oregano leaves,
plus a few extra to serve
2 tbsp extra virgin olive oil
85g feta cheese, crumbled

Serves 4

Peel the grapefruit, removing all the skin and pith. Segment the grapefruit, place in a bowl and squeeze over the juice from the membranes.

Bring a pan of salted water to the boil and blanch the courgettes for 3 minutes, until just tender. Drain well and add to the grapefruit segments and juice, along with the spring onions, oregano leaves and extra virgin olive oil.

Season the lamb fillets well with sea salt and black pepper. Heat the oil in a frying pan and brown the lamb on both sides, then lower the heat and cook for a further 2 - 3 minutes on each side. Remove from the pan and leave to rest for a few minutes.

Divide the courgette and grapefruit salad between four plates, holding back some of the dressing. Thickly slice the lamb and place on top of the salad. Crumble the feta over the top, scatter with the extra oregano leaves, drizzle with the remaining dressing and serve immediately.

Three shepherds work on the Chatsworth estate and with the help of seasonal workers they look after more than six thousand lambs including Texel, Suffolk and Rouge de L'Ouest cross breeds.

Ben Randles,
Head Shepherd, Chatsworth

Fillet of Beef with Aubergine,
Tomato and Basil Compote

First make the compote, which can be prepared 24 hours in advance. Heat the olive oil in a large sauté pan, add the aubergine and cook for 5 - 10 minutes until golden brown. Add the tomatoes and cook for a further 5 - 10 minutes until the tomatoes have split and softened. Add the garlic and thyme and cook, stirring, for 2 minutes, then add the balsamic vinegar. Bubble until the liquid has reduced and the compote is thick. Roughly tear in the basil leaves, season well with sea salt and black pepper and leave to cool. The compote is best served at room temperature.

Heat a heavy-based griddle or frying pan until smoking. Brush the steaks with the oil and season well with sea salt and black pepper. Cook on the hot griddle for 2 - 3 minutes each side for rare steaks, or 4 minutes each side for medium. Remove the steaks from the pan and leave to rest for a couple of minutes before serving with a spoonful of the compote.

4 x 200g fillet steaks
1 tbsp vegetable
or rapeseed oil

For the compote
50ml olive oil
1 aubergine, diced
200g cherry tomatoes, halved
2 cloves garlic,
peeled and crushed
1 tsp thyme leaves
1 tbsp balsamic vinegar
Small bunch basil

Serves 4

Summer

Herb-Crusted Rack of Lamb
with Pea, Mint and Shallot Sauce

Heat 1 tablespoon of the olive oil in a heavy based frying pan and brown the racks of lamb on all sides. Remove from the pan and place in a roasting tin. Mix the breadcrumbs with the chopped herbs and season with sea salt and black pepper. Spread each rack of lamb with a little mustard and press the herb breadcrumbs on top. Mix the melted butter with the other tablespoon of oil and drizzle this over the herb-crusted meat. Roast in the preheated oven for 12 - 15 minutes, then turn the oven down to 180°C/350°F/Gas Mark 4 and cook for a further 5 minutes.

Meanwhile, prepare the pea sauce. Melt the butter in a saucepan and add the shallots. Cook over a gentle heat for 5 - 10 minutes, until softened, then add the frozen peas and stir well to coat in the buttery juices. Add the vegetable stock and bring to the boil. Simmer for 3 - 4 minutes, then remove from the heat and add the cream and mint. Season and purée with a hand blender.

Remove the lamb from the oven and leave to rest for a few minutes before serving with the pea, mint and shallot sauce.

4 x 3 bone racks of lamb, French trimmed
100g fine fresh breadcrumbs
1 tbsp parsley, finely chopped
1 tbsp basil, finely chopped
½ tbsp rosemary, finely chopped
2 tbsp Dijon mustard
50g butter, melted
2 tbsp olive oil

For the sauce
50g butter
2 shallots, peeled and finely diced
350g frozen peas
100ml vegetable stock
1 tbsp double cream
2 tbsp mint, finely chopped

Serves 4

Preheat the oven to
200°C/400°F/Gas Mark 6

Chicory Caesar Salad
with Seared Tiger Prawns

Whisk together the olive oil and crushed garlic. Cut the pitta bread into 2cm cubes and toss in half of the garlicky oil. Place on a baking sheet and cook in the preheated oven for 8 - 10 minutes, until golden brown and crisp. Remove from the oven and leave to cool.

Next make the dressing. Combine the mayonnaise, cream, lemon juice and anchovy essence in a bowl. Stir in the crushed garlic and Parmesan cheese and season to taste. If the dressing is too thick, add a little more lemon juice or a dash of warm water. Cut the root ends off the chicory and separate into individual leaves. Rinse, drain and set aside.

Place the remaining garlicky oil in a large frying pan over a high heat, until sizzling. Add the tiger prawns and sear for a minute on each side. You may have to do this in a few batches to avoid over-crowding the pan and lowering the temperature.

Arrange the chicory on a platter or salad bowl. Scatter over the croutons, arrange the seared prawns on top and drizzle over the Caesar dressing. Use a potato peeler to peel shavings of Parmesan cheese over the top and sprinkle with the chives. Serve immediately.

3 tbsp olive oil
1 clove garlic,
peeled and crushed
2 pitta breads
4 heads white chicory
300g raw tiger prawns,
peeled
25g Parmesan cheese
Small bunch chives,
finely chopped

For the dressing
250ml good quality
mayonnaise
3 tbsp double cream
½ lemon, juiced
½ tsp anchovy essence
2 garlic cloves,
peeled and crushed
2 tbsp Parmesan cheese,
grated

Serves 4

Preheat the oven to
190°C/375°F/Gas Mark 5

Summer

Sticky Pork Kebabs
with a Sweet Carrot Coleslaw

Mix together the rapeseed oil, soy sauce, ketchup, Chinese five spice, orange zest and juice. Season with black pepper and add the pork, coating it well in the mixture. Marinade for one to two hours.

For the coleslaw, grate or finely shred the carrots. Finely shred the red and white cabbage and mix together with the carrots, bean sprouts and spring onions. Mix together the mayonnaise and sweet chilli sauce, season and use this to dress the coleslaw.

Thread the diced pork onto wooden skewers which have been soaked in water to prevent them scorching. Cook in the preheated oven for 20 minutes, turning regularly until the pork is cooked through and the kebabs are sticky and glazed.

Serve the kebabs with the sweet carrot coleslaw on the side.

**500g loin of pork,
diced into large cubes
2 tbsp rapeseed oil
1 tbsp dark soy sauce
3 tbsp tomato ketchup
½ tsp Chinese five spice
1 orange, zested and juiced**

For the coleslaw
**250g carrots, peeled
150g red cabbage
150g white cabbage
85g bean sprouts
3 spring onions,
finely sliced
3 tbsp mayonnaise
2 tbsp sweet chilli sauce**

Serves 4

Preheat the oven to
200°C/400°F/Gas Mark 6

Chicken and Bacon Terrine
with Fresh Peach Chutney

700g chicken breast meat,
finely diced
2 tbsp olive oil
150ml port
1 onion, peeled
and finely chopped
2 cloves garlic,
peeled and crushed
1 tsp thyme leaves
1 lemon, zested
3 large bay leaves
10 rashers
smoked streaky bacon
450g chicken livers,
roughly chopped

For the peach chutney
1.8kg peaches, peeled,
stoned and cut into large
pieces
180g soft light brown sugar
1 onion, peeled and finely
chopped
1 tbsp coriander seeds
1 tsp ground ginger
¼ tsp salt
290ml white wine vinegar

Serves 6 - 8

Preheat the oven to
170°C/325°F/Gas Mark 3

For the peach chutney, place all the ingredients in a large, heavy-based saucepan and bring slowly to the boil. Simmer gently for 30 - 45 minutes, until tender and thick. Pour into warmed, sterilised jars and seal.

For the terrine, place the olive oil, port, onion, garlic, thyme and lemon zest in a small saucepan and bring to the boil. Simmer for 5 minutes, then turn off the heat and leave to cool.

Place the diced chicken in a large bowl and pour over the cold marinade. Leave for several hours or overnight if possible.

Line a 2lb loaf tin with cling film and lay the bay leaves in the bottom. Stretch the bacon rashers with the back of a knife, then lay them into the loaf tin widthways so that they are overlapping and there is some bacon hanging over either side.

Add the chicken livers to the marinaded chicken, season well with sea salt and black pepper and mix thoroughly. Pack this mixture into the lined loaf tin and fold the bacon over the top. Cover the top of the loaf tin tightly with tin foil and stand in a roasting tin. Pour in boiling water to half way up the sides of the loaf tin and place in the preheated oven for 2 hours.

Remove the tin from the oven and allow to cool. Once cool, press with a weight and chill overnight. To serve, turn the terrine out and return to room temperature, before cutting into slices and serving with the fresh peach chutney.

Griddled Balsamic Steak
with Beetroot Salad and Horseradish Cream

Marinade the steaks in the olive oil, balsamic vinegar, red wine, red onions and thyme for at least 2 hours.

For the horseradish cream, mix together the crème fraiche and horseradish and season with sea salt and black pepper. When ready to use, stir through the diced beetroot.

For the salad, mix together all the ingredients and toss in the extra virgin olive oil.

Remove the steaks from the marinade, reserving the onions and the liquid. Season the steaks, heat a ridged griddle pan until smoking hot and griddle the steaks with the red onion until cooked to your liking. Remove the steaks to a plate to rest, turn down the heat and add the marinade to the pan. Divide the salad between four plates and place the steak on top. Drizzle over the red onion with the marinade juices and top with a spoonful of the horseradish cream. Serve immediately.

4 x 200g sirloin steaks
4 tbsp olive oil
2 tbsp balsamic vinegar
1 tbsp red wine
1 red onion,
peeled and sliced
1 sprig thyme

For the beetroot salad
4 cooked beetroot,
sliced and cut into strips
200g cherry tomatoes, halved
1 bunch spring onions,
trimmed and finely sliced
½ red chilli,
deseeded and finely diced
2 large handfuls ruby chard
1 bunch coriander,
roughly chopped
1 tbsp extra virgin olive oil

For the horseradish cream
2 tbsp crème fraiche
1 tbsp creamed horseradish
½ cooked beetroot,
finely diced

Serves 4

Jim Howson's free-range chickens are allowed to grow naturally, enjoying a GM-free diet without hormones, growth promoters or added fats, while they happily roam around his beautiful farm in Bradley, Derbyshire.

Jim Howson
Derbyshire Dales Chickens,
Common End Farm, Derbyshire

Summer

New Potato and Asparagus Salad
with Shallots, Dovedale Blue Cheese and Basil

Bring a large pan of salted water to the boil and add the new potatoes. Cover and cook for 20 minutes until the potatoes are just cooked through. Lift out the potatoes, cool under cold running water, drain well and cut into quarters.

Return the pan to the heat and bring back to the boil. Add the asparagus and blanch for 4 minutes, until it is just tender. Drain and refresh under cold running water to keep the bright green colour.

Place the potatoes in a large bowl and dress with the extra virgin olive oil and lemon juice. Add the shallots, cherry tomatoes, olives and most of the basil and toss well together. Crumble in the Dovedale Blue cheese and season with black pepper (the olives and blue cheese should provide plenty of salt).

Add the asparagus and pile the salad into a serving bowl. Garnish with the remaining basil and serve.

225g British new potatoes
2 bundles British asparagus
4 tbsp extra virgin olive oil
1 tbsp lemon juice
2 shallots,
peeled and finely sliced
250g cherry tomatoes, halved
50g black olives,
stoned and roughly chopped
150g Dovedale Blue cheese
1 bunch basil,
finely shredded

Serves 4

Summer

Summer

puddings

Eton Mess
with Strawberries and Raspberries

First make the meringue. Line a baking sheet with baking parchment or silicone paper.

Place the egg whites in a large metal or glass bowl and whisk with electric beaters to stiff peaks. Add the caster sugar in five or six additions, whisking all the time. The meringue should be stiff and shiny. Place spoonfuls of the meringue onto the lined baking sheet and bake at the bottom of the preheated oven for an hour, or until the meringue is crisp and lifts away from the paper. Remove from the oven and leave to cool. Once cool, break up into pieces.

Whip the cream with the icing sugar, Grand Marnier and orange zest to soft peaks. Quarter or halve the strawberries, depending on their size. Fold together the cream, strawberries, raspberries and meringue pieces and serve in glasses or bowls, garnished with a sprig of mint.

2 egg whites
110g caster sugar
750ml double cream
100g icing sugar
1 tbsp Grand Marnier
1 orange, zested
150g strawberries, hulled
150g raspberries
4 mint sprigs, to garnish

Serves 4

Preheat the oven to
140°C/275°F/Gas Mark 1

Summer

Lavender Cake

Grease a loaf tin and line the bottom with greaseproof paper.

Cream together the butter and caster sugar until pale and fluffy. Add the eggs, one at a time, beating well after each addition, then beat in the lemon zest. Sift in the flour and fold into the mixture, then fold in the ground almonds and lavender flowers. Spoon the mixture into the greased loaf tin and bake in the preheated oven for 40 minutes, until well risen, golden brown and firm to the touch. Remove from the oven and leave to cool in the tin for 10 minutes before turning out onto a wire rack.

For the icing, place the granulated sugar in a small saucepan with the water and heat gently until the sugar has dissolved. Add the lavender and simmer for 2 minutes. Leave the syrup to cool and infuse. Sift the icing sugar into a bowl and strain over the syrup. Mix well, adding more icing sugar or syrup as necessary to achieve the consistency of thick icing. Drizzle the icing over the cake and decorate with the sprigs of lavender.

For the cake
110g unsalted butter, softened
110g caster sugar
2 large eggs
1 lemon, zested
110g self-raising flour
25g ground almonds
1 tbsp lavender flowers, removed from stalk

For the icing
3 tbsp granulated sugar
3 tbsp water
6 sprigs lavender
300g icing sugar
Lavender sprigs, to decorate

Serves 8

Preheat the oven to 180°C/350°F/Gas Mark 4

Summer

Nectarine and Raspberry Pudding
with Amaretti Biscuits

4 nectarines
110g caster sugar
150ml water
1 vanilla pod
200g raspberries
575ml double cream
3 - 4 tbsp icing sugar
2 tbsp Amaretto
16 Amaretti biscuits,
crushed,
plus extra to serve

Serves 4

Place the sugar and water in a saucepan and heat gently to dissolve the sugar. Halve the vanilla pod and add to the pan. Halve and stone the nectarines and add to the pan. Poach gently for 10 - 15 minutes, until the nectarines are tender, then lift them out into a bowl and boil the liquid until syrupy. Slip the skins off the nectarines and pour over the vanilla syrup. Leave to cool.

Place the double cream and icing sugar in a large bowl and lightly whip into soft peaks. Fold through the Amaretto.

Assemble the pudding, either in four deep glasses or in a glass bowl. Layer up the Amaretto cream, nectarines, raspberries and crushed Amaretti biscuits, finishing with a scattering of Amaretti crumbs. Garnish with a sprig of mint and serve with extra Amaretti biscuits on the side.

puddings

Gooseberry and Elderflower Cheesecake

Butter the bottom and sides of a 20cm springform cake tin.

Crush the biscuits in a food processor, or place in a plastic bag and crush with a rolling pin. Melt the butter with the golden syrup, add the biscuit crumbs and stir until well combined. Press into the base of the cake tin and refrigerate for 30 minutes, or until the base is solid.

Place the mascarpone and cream cheese in a large bowl, add the sugar and beat until smooth. Fold in the cream, egg yolks, vanilla and lemon juice. Spoon this on top of the base, making sure there are no air pockets.

Place the gooseberries, sugar and elderflower cordial in a large saucepan and cook very gently for 10 minutes. The gooseberries should be tender but still whole. Leave to cool in the syrup. Once cool, arrange the gooseberries on top of the cheesecake. Refrigerate for at least 2 hours, or overnight.

Release the springform tin and slide the cheesecake onto a serving plate. Dust with icing sugar and serve, cut into wedges.

For the base
100g Hobnobs
or sweet oat biscuits
150g gingernut biscuits
50g unsalted butter, plus
extra for greasing
1 tbsp golden syrup

For the filling
500g mascarpone cheese
100g cream cheese
100g caster sugar
290ml double cream, lightly whipped
2 egg yolks
1 tsp vanilla extract
1 tsp lemon juice
500g gooseberries, topped and tailed
100g caster sugar
4 tbsp elderflower cordial

Serves 6 - 8

Summer

Quick Brioche Summer Pudding
with Berry and Elderflower Coulis

400g brioche loaf
200g strawberries, hulled
100g raspberries
100g redcurrants
100g blueberries
25g caster sugar

For the coulis
100g redcurrants
100g blackcurrants
200g raspberries
180g caster sugar
150ml water
2 tbsp elderflower cordial
1 lemon, juiced

Serves 4

First make the berry and elderflower coulis. Place the fruit, sugar and water in a saucepan and bring to the boil. Simmer for 2 minutes, then purée and sieve. Stir in the elderflower cordial and lemon juice to taste.

Halve the strawberries, or quarter them if they are large and mix with the raspberries, redcurrants, blueberries and caster sugar. Cut the crusts off the brioche loaf and slice thickly. Stamp out eight rounds of brioche using a 6cm cutter.

Dip one of the brioche rounds into the coulis so that it is well coated and place in the middle of a pudding plate. Place a pile of fruit on top, then top with another dipped brioche round. Repeat this process on the other three plates. Spoon any remaining fruit around the summer puddings and drizzle with the remaining coulis. Dust with icing sugar and serve with double cream or vanilla icecream.

Summer

Autumn

to start

Twice Baked Lincolnshire Poacher
Soufflé with Apple Chutney

For the chutney, place all the ingredients in a large preserving pan and slowly bring to the boil. Simmer gently for 15 - 20 minutes, until tender and thick. Set aside to cool, or if storing, pour immediately into warmed, sterilised jars and seal.

Butter the bottom and sides of four ramekins and coat with the breadcrumbs.

Melt the butter in a saucepan and stir in the flour. Cook for 2 minutes, stirring constantly, then gradually blend in the milk. Bring to the boil and simmer for 2 minutes until the sauce has thickened. Remove from the heat and add half the Lincolnshire Poacher and the egg yolks. Season well with sea salt and black pepper.

In a separate bowl, whisk the egg whites with a pinch of salt to medium peaks. Mix a tablespoonful of egg white into the base mixture and stir until well combined, then gently fold through the remainder. Half fill the ramekins with the soufflé mixture, sprinkle with the remaining cheese, then cover with the rest of the mixture. Smooth the surface with a spatula, then run your thumb around the inside edge of the ramekins so that they can rise evenly. Place the ramekins in a roasting tin and pour in boiling water to come half way up the ramekins. Bake in the preheated oven for 15 minutes, until risen and golden.

Leave the soufflés in the ramekins until cool enough to handle, then turn out onto individual oven proof plates. To serve, turn the oven up to 200°C/400°F/Gas Mark 6. Return the soufflés to the oven for 10 - 12 minutes, until puffed up and golden and serve with the apple chutney.

30g unsalted butter
30g plain white flour
290ml milk
2 egg yolks
85g Lincolnshire Poacher cheese, grated
4 egg whites

To prepare the ramekins
30g unsalted butter
50g fine white breadcrumbs

For the apple chutney
4 cooking apples, peeled, cored and cut into pieces
1 onion,
peeled and finely chopped
225g soft light brown sugar
110g raisins
1 tsp dry mustard powder
1 tsp salt
1 tsp curry powder
½ tsp ground ginger
1 tbsp golden syrup
225ml cider vinegar

Serves 4

Preheat the oven to
180°C/350°F/Gas Mark 4

Autumn

Pheasant Paté
with Whisky and Thyme

1 pheasant
60ml whisky
6 crushed juniper berries
1 tsp thyme leaves
1 carrot, roughly chopped
1 onion,
peeled and roughly chopped
1 leek, trimmed
and roughly chopped
85g butter
2 rashers streaky bacon,
finely chopped
55g pork fat, mince
2 shallots,
peeled and finely chopped
1 clove garlic,
peeled and crushed
1 tsp redcurrant jelly

For the top
55g unsalted butter
4 sprigs thyme

Serves 4

Remove the pheasant breasts with a sharp knife. Place in a dish and pour over the whisky, juniper berries and thyme leaves and leave to marinate for 2 hours. Place the carcass in a large saucepan with the carrot, onion and leek and cover with cold water. Bring to the boil and simmer for 2 hours. Strain the stock and boil rapidly to reduce to 100ml.

Remove the pheasant from the marinade, pat dry and cut into dice. Melt the butter in a frying pan and sauté the pheasant until just cooked. Remove from the pan and set aside to cool. Add the bacon, pork fat and shallots. Cook for 10 minutes, until the bacon is cooked and the shallots are soft. Add the garlic and redcurrant jelly and cook for a further 2 minutes. Leave to cool.

Place the pheasant in a food processor along with the bacon and shallot mixture and process until finely ground. Tip into a bowl and add the reduced stock. Divide the mixture between four ramekins and press down firmly. Melt the unsalted butter and pour a layer over the top of each ramekin. Lay a sprig of thyme on top and press down so that it is just covered by the butter. Chill until set. Serve with plenty of warm bread.

The pheasants that live in the woodlands at Chatsworth have been looked after for generations by dedicated gamekeepers.

Chatsworth gamekeepers
Steven Read and Paul Tooley

Buxton Blue and Courgette Fritters
with Pear Relish

For the relish, place all the ingredients in a saucepan and cook over a gentle heat for 15 minutes, until reduced and thickened.

Bring a large pan of salted water to the boil and blanch the courgettes for 1 minute. Drain and refresh under cold running water. Pat dry and mix with the blue cheese, flour, milk and egg yolks. Season well with black pepper. Whisk the egg whites to soft peaks and fold carefully into the courgette mixture.

Heat the oil in a large frying pan to a depth of 1cm and fry spoonfuls of the mixture until golden brown on each side. Drain well on kitchen paper and serve with the pear relish.

For the fritters

400g courgettes, finely diced
200g Buxton Blue cheese, crumbled
65g plain flour
1 tbsp milk
3 egg yolks
2 egg whites
Vegetable oil, for frying

For the pear relish

3 Conference pears, peeled, cored and chopped into 2cm pieces
1 small onion, peeled and finely chopped
2 tbsp white wine vinegar
85g soft dark brown sugar

Serves 4

Roasted Pepper and Pumpkin Soup

**4 red peppers, deseeded
and cut into quarters
30g butter
1 tbsp olive oil
1 onion,
peeled and finely chopped
750g pumpkin,
peeled and diced
1 red chilli, deseeded
and finely chopped
4 cloves garlic,
peeled and crushed
1 litre vegetable stock
150ml double cream**

To serve
**50g Greek yoghurt
2 tsp chives, finely chopped
30g pumpkin seeds,
toasted**

Serves 4

Preheat the oven to
200°C/400°F/Gas Mark 6

Place the peppers, skin side up, on a baking sheet and roast in the preheated oven for 20 - 25 minutes, until the skins are charred. Remove from the oven and place in a bowl. Cover with cling film and leave to cool. Once cool, peel off the skins.

Meanwhile, melt the butter with the oil in a large, heavy-based saucepan. Add the onion, pumpkin and red chilli, season with sea salt and black pepper and sweat the vegetables for 5 - 10 minutes without browning. Add the garlic and cook on a low heat for a further minute. Pour in the vegetable stock, bring to the boil and simmer gently for 15 minutes. Add in the red peppers and cook for a further 5 minutes.

Blend the soup in a food processor or with a hand blender and adjust the seasoning to taste. Return to the pan and stir in the cream. Gently reheat the soup and ladle into warmed bowls. Place a spoonful of Greek yoghurt in each and sprinkle with the chives and toasted pumpkin seeds.

to start

Warm Salad of Pigeon
with Black Pudding, Green Beans and Walnuts

First make the dressing. Whisk together the walnut oil, white wine vinegar, mustard and caster sugar with the shallot, garlic and parsley, set aside.

Heat the olive oil in a large frying pan, add the pigeon breasts and black pudding and sear on both sides. Reduce the heat and cook for 3 - 4 minutes, until the pigeon is cooked, but still pink in the middle. Remove the pigeon and leave to rest in a warm place. Add the walnuts to the pan and fry for 1 minute, then remove the walnuts and black pudding and reserve. Add the dressing to the pan and heat until warmed through.

Carve the pigeon breasts into slices. Arrange the salad leaves and green beans on four plates, top with the pigeon and black pudding, scatter over the walnuts and drizzle with the warm dressing. Garnish with some chopped parsley and serve.

8 breasts wood pigeon
2 tbsp olive oil
100g black pudding, sliced
200g green beans, trimmed,
blanched and refreshed
50g walnut halves
Selection of salad leaves,
to serve

For the dressing
4 tbsp walnut oil
2 tbsp white wine vinegar
½ tbsp Dijon mustard
½ tsp caster sugar
1 shallot,
peeled and finely chopped
2 cloves garlic,
peeled and crushed
1 tbsp parsley,
finely chopped,
plus extra to garnish

Serves 4

Autumn

Autumn

main courses

Fillet of Beef
with a Ragout of Wild Mushrooms

Roughly grind the peppercorns in a pestle and mortar and press over the surface of the beef. Season with sea salt. Melt 15g of the butter with the oil in a large sauté pan. Over a high heat, quickly brown the beef fillet on all sides. Remove to a roasting tin and cook in the preheated oven for 15 - 20 minutes for rare meat, or longer according to taste.

Melt the remaining butter in the pan and add the onion. Cover and cook over a gentle heat for 10 minutes, until the onion is soft and translucent. Turn up the heat slightly and add the wild mushrooms. Sauté for 5 - 10 minutes, until the mushrooms have released their liquid. Continue to cook until the liquid has evaporated.

Add the garlic and rosemary and cook for a further 2 minutes, then pour in the white wine and stock. Simmer and reduce for 5 minutes before adding the double cream and simmering until the liquid has thickened and coats the mushrooms. Remove from the heat and stir in the grated parmesan cheese. Adjust the seasoning to taste.

Remove the beef from the oven and leave to rest for 5 - 10 minutes before carving and serving with the wild mushroom ragout.

1.2 kg fillet of beef
1 tbsp cracked
black peppercorns
45g butter
1 tbsp oil
2 onions,
peeled and finely diced
500g wild mushrooms,
wiped clean and sliced
1 tsp rosemary,
finely chopped
2 garlic cloves,
peeled and crushed
150ml white wine
200ml beef
or chicken stock
200ml double cream
50g Parmesan cheese,
grated

Serves 4

Preheat the oven to
200°C/400°F/Gas Mark 6

Autumn

Autumn Vegetable Tagine
with Squash, Carrots and Apricots

Heat the oil in a large casserole dish and add the onion. Cover and cook for 5 minutes, until the onion is starting to soften. Add the butternut squash, carrots and sweet potato, replace the lid and cook for a further 5 minutes.

Next add the apricots, chilli and garlic and cook, stirring, for 2 minutes, then stir in the spices. Cook for 2 minutes, until the spices smell toasted, then pour in the saffron with its soaking liquid and add the tomatoes. Blend in the stock, season and simmer for 15 minutes, until the vegetables are almost tender.

Add the peas and cook for a further five minutes. Stir in the coriander and parsley and serve with couscous.

1 onion, diced
3 tbsp olive oil
500g butternut squash, peeled and diced
500g carrots, peeled and diced
1 sweet potato, peeled and diced
20 dried apricots
1 red chilli, deseeded and finely chopped
2 cloves garlic, peeled and crushed
½ tsp ground ginger
1 tsp cumin seeds
1 tsp ground coriander
1 tsp ground cumin
1 cinnamon stick
½ tsp saffron soaked in 50ml warm water
4 tomatoes skinned and roughly chopped
100ml chicken or vegetable stock
300g frozen peas
Small bunch coriander, finely chopped
Small bunch parsley, finely chopped

Serves 4

Autumn

Lincolnshire Sausage Cassoulet
with Flageolet Beans and Garlic Crostini

Heat the oil in a frying pan and brown the sausages on all sides. Remove from the pan and reserve. Add the shallots, carrots and celery to the pan and sauté for 5 minutes, then add the garlic, rosemary and bay leaf and cook for a further minute.

Add the wine and stock, bring to the boil, then add the flageolet beans, tomatoes and redcurrant jelly. Return the sausages to the pan and simmer for 30 - 40 minutes, until the sauce has thickened and the beans are soft and cooked through. Add the olives and cook for a further five minutes. Check the seasoning, remembering the olives are salty and adjust as necessary.

For the crostini, mix together the crushed garlic and softened butter and season with sea salt and black pepper. Spread the the garlic butter onto both sides of the baguette slices and grill each side until golden.

Sprinkle the parsley over the cassoulet and serve with the garlic crostini.

8 Lincolnshire sausages
1 tbsp olive oil
8 shallots,
peeled and left whole
1 carrot, peeled and diced
1 stick celery, diced
1 garlic clove,
peeled and crushed
1 sprig rosemary
1 bay leaf
100ml white wine
150ml chicken stock
250g fresh flageolet beans
2 tins chopped tomatoes
1 tbsp redcurrant jelly
50g pitted olives
1tbsp parsley,
finely chopped

For the garlic crostini
8 slices baguette
60g butter, softened
2 cloves garlic,
peeled and crushed

Serves 4

Autumn

Roast Partridge
with Glazed Turnips, Shallots and Smoked Bacon

**4 partridges (young English
ones if possible)**
30g butter
12 small shallots, peeled
**6 rashers smoked streaky
bacon, sliced**
**250g small white turnips,
peeled and quartered**
1 tsp caster sugar
50ml white wine
2 sprigs thyme
**1 tbsp parsley,
finely chopped**

Serves 4

Heat half the butter in a pan and brown the partridges well on
all sides. Remove from the pan and reserve. Wipe out the pan
and then add the remaining butter. Add the shallots, bacon and
turnips and sauté for 10 minutes, until golden brown. Add the
caster sugar and cook for a further 2 minutes, until glazed and
caramelised. Season and add the white wine, 2 tablespoons
of water and the thyme. Place the partridges on top, cover and
cook over a gentle heat for 20 - 25 minutes, until the partridges
are tender and cooked through.

Remove the partridges from the pan and bring the liquid to the
boil. Boil for a couple of minutes, until the liquid is well reduced
and coating the vegetables. Add the parsley and adjust the
seasoning to taste. Carve or joint the partridges and serve
with the glazed turnips, shallots and smoked bacon and some
creamy mashed potatoes.

main courses

Rabbit with Pears, Prunes and Bay Leaves

Dust the rabbit pieces with the flour and season with sea salt and black pepper. Heat the olive oil in a large, heavy based pan or casserole and brown the rabbit on all sides. Set aside. Add the onion to the pan, cover and cook for 10 minutes on a gentle heat, until soft and translucent.

Add the wine, stock, balsamic vinegar, brown sugar, bay leaves and rosemary and season with sea salt and black pepper. Return the rabbit to the pan, bring to a simmer, cover and cook on a low heat for 30 minutes.

Add the pears and prunes to the pan, cover and simmer for a further 30 minutes. Remove the rabbit, pears and prunes from the pan and arrange on plates or a serving dish. Remove the bay leaves and rosemary from the pan and whisk the butter into the hot sauce until slightly thickened and glossy, spoon the sauce over the rabbit and serve.

2 young rabbits, each jointed into 4 pieces
3 tbsp plain flour
3 tbsp olive oil
1 onion,
peeled and finely chopped
300ml red wine
100ml chicken stock
2 tbsp balsamic vinegar
1 tbsp brown sugar
2 bay leaves
2 sprigs fresh rosemary
2 pears, slightly under ripe,
peeled, cored and halved
8 prunes
50g butter, cubed
and chilled

Serves 4

Baked Chicken
with Lemon, Carrots, Garlic and Potatoes

Coat a large, ovenproof dish liberally with the butter. Layer the potatoes and garlic on the bottom of the dish and season well, then add the carrots. Slice one of the lemons into thin slices and scatter over the carrots. Add the herbs, drizzle with the olive oil and pour over 2 tablespoons of water. Cover with foil and bake in the preheated oven for 35 - 40 minutes, until the vegetables are starting to soften.

Remove the dish from the oven and discard the foil. Lay the chicken pieces on top of the vegetables, skin side up and squeeze over the juice from the second lemon. Drizzle over the remaining olive oil and return to the oven for 25 - 30 minutes. Remove from the oven, baste with the pan juices and cook for a further 5 minutes until the chicken is well browned and the skin is crisp.

Serve the chicken and vegetables with extra lemon wedges on the side.

**4 chicken thighs and
4 chicken drumsticks
20g butter, softened
4 medium potatoes,
3 cloves garlic,
peeled and finely sliced
500g carrots, peeled and
cut into batons
peeled and cut into slices
2 lemons
2 sprigs fresh rosemary
2 sprigs fresh thyme
3 tbsp olive oil**

Serves 4

Preheat the oven to
200ºC/400ºF/Gas Mark 6

Autumn

Venison Burger
with Blue Cheese and Crispy Shallots

Place the venison in a large bowl and season well. Gently mix in the cream, garlic, herbs and juniper berries until well combined. Shape the mixture into 4 patties. Make an indentation in the top of each one. Divide the cheese into 4 portions and shape each one into a ball. Push the cheese into the centre of each burger and cover well with the meat so that the cheese is sealed in. Chill for an hour.

Meanwhile, heat 2 tablespoons of the olive oil in a frying pan and add the shallots. Cook over a medium heat for 5 - 10 minutes, until crispy. Remove from the pan and drain well on kitchen paper.

Preheat a heavy ridged griddle pan until very hot. Add the remaining olive oil and sear the burgers to seal in the juices. Turn down the heat and cook for 2 - 3 minutes on each side, so that the cheese melts in the middle and the burgers are medium rare.

Serve the burgers on lightly toasted bread rolls with the crispy shallots on top.

650g venison mince
5 tbsp double cream
2 cloves garlic, peeled and crushed
½ tbsp flat leaved parsley, finely chopped
½ tbsp chives, finely chopped
4 juniper berries, crushed
110g blue cheese
3 tbsp olive oil
12 shallots, peeled and thinly sliced into rings

Serves 4

Autumn

Creamy Cider and Mustard Pork
with Spinach

4 pork loin steaks / chops
1 tbsp rapeseed oil
2 red apples, cored and cut
into wedges
200ml dry cider
200g crème fraiche
1 tbsp good quality
wholegrain mustard
225g baby leaf spinach

Serves 4

Heat the rapeseed oil in a large, deep frying pan over a medium to high heat. Season the pork and brown for 2 minutes each side. Remove from the pan and keep warm. Add the apple wedges and cook for 2 - 3 minutes, stirring, until golden. Remove from the pan and keep warm with the pork.

Keep the pan on the heat and pour in the cider. Bring to the boil and reduce by half, then reduce the heat slightly and stir in the crème fraiche and wholegrain mustard. Return the pork to the pan, along with any juices. Simmer for 4 minutes, turning the meat halfway, then add the apple wedges and cook for a further minute.

Place the pork and apples onto warmed serving plates. Stir the baby leaf spinach into the sauce and cook until wilted. Season well and serve the sauce and spinach alongside the pork.

David Wainwright, holder of the Peak District Environmental Quality Mark, shows that not only does he care for his pigs, he cares for the environment too.

David and Ann Wainwright, Dove Top Farm, Cold Eaton, Ashbourne.

Chatsworth Wild Boar
with Apples, Blackberries and Sage

Rub the sage into the wild boar steaks and season. Melt half the butter with the olive oil in a large frying pan and pan fry the steaks for 3 minutes on each side, depending on their thickness, or until they are cooked to your liking. Remove the meat from the pan and place in a low oven to keep warm.

Melt the remaining butter in the pan and add the shallots and apples. Cook for 5 minutes over a very gentle heat, until the shallots have softened. Turn up the heat and add the caster sugar. Stir the shallots and apples and cook until lightly caramelised.

Pour in the white wine and bring to the boil. Add the redcurrant jelly and reduce slightly before adding the double cream and reducing again until the sauce is of a light coating consistency. Adjust the seasoning to taste and add the blackberries. Simmer until the blackberries are heated through and serve the apples, blackberries and sauce alongside the wild boar steaks.

4 wild boar steaks
1 tbsp sage, finely chopped
30g butter
1 tbsp olive oil
2 shallots,
peeled and finely diced
3 rosy English apples,
cored and cut into 6
1 tsp caster sugar
150ml white wine
1 tbsp redcurrant jelly
150ml double cream
110g blackberries

Serves 4

Autumn

Warm Chorizo, Broccoli, Pea and Feta Tart

First make the pastry. Sift the flour with the salt into the bowl of a food processor. Add the diced, chilled butter and pulse until the mixture resembles fine breadcrumbs. Tip into a large bowl and stir in the grated cheese. Sprinkle over a couple of tablespoonfuls of cold water and stir until the mixture comes together. Roll out the pastry and use to line a 20cm loose bottomed flan tin. Chill for 30 minutes, or until the pastry is solid. Line the pastry case with a circle of greaseproof paper, fill with baking beans and bake blind for 15 minutes. Remove the beans and bake for a further 5 minutes until the pastry is dry and biscuity. Turn the oven down to 170°C/325°F/Gas Mark 3.

Arrange the broccoli, peas, chorizo and feta in the pastry case. Beat together the whole eggs, egg yolks and double cream and season. Pour this into the pastry case and return the tart to the oven. Cook for 25 - 30 minutes, until the tart has just set. Remove from the oven and leave to cool slightly. Serve warm, with a green salad.

For the pastry
225g plain flour
110g butter,
chilled and diced
50g mature cheddar, grated
Cold water to bind

For the filling
300g frozen peas, blanched,
drained and refreshed
100g broccoli, blanched,
drained and refreshed
80g chorizo sausage,
thinly sliced
200g feta, crumbled
3 whole eggs
2 egg yolks
200ml double cream

Serves 6 - 8

Preheat the oven to
200°C/400°F/Gas Mark 5

Autumn

puddings

Walnut Treacle Tart

First make the pastry. Sift together the flour, salt and icing sugar. Rub in the cold butter using a food processor or your fingertips until the mixture resembles fine breadcrumbs. Mix the egg yolk with the cold water and add to the mixture to bring together. Shape the pastry into a flat disc and chill in the fridge for half an hour. Roll out the pastry and use to line a 20cm loose bottomed tart tin. Chill for half an hour or until the pastry is solid.

Line the pastry case with a circle of greaseproof paper, fill with baking beans and bake blind for 15 minutes. Remove the beans and bake for a further 5 minutes until the pastry is dry and biscuity. Remove from the oven and leave to cool. Turn the oven down to 170°C/325°F/Gas Mark 3.

Next prepare the filling. Melt the butter with the golden syrup in a saucepan and leave to cool to room temperature before whisking in the double cream and eggs until well mixed. Scatter the walnut halves over the base of the pastry case. Pour the filling on top and bake in the preheated oven for 30 - 40 minutes, until the tart is set.

Serve the tart warm, dusted with icing sugar, with cream or icecream.

For the pastry
180g plain flour
Pinch of salt
40g icing sugar
125g unsalted butter, chilled and diced
1 large egg yolk
2 tablespoons cold water

For the filling
55g unsalted butter
6 tbsp golden syrup
2 tbsp double cream
2 large eggs, beaten
75g walnut halves
Icing sugar, to serve

Serves 6 - 8

Preheat the oven to
200°C/400°F/Gas Mark 6

Autumn

Damson Crème Brûlée

8 egg yolks
1 pint double cream
1 tsp natural vanilla extract
85g caster sugar
200g damsons
55g caster sugar
Icing sugar, to caramelise

Serves 4

Halve and stone the damsons and place in a saucepan with the sugar and a splash of water. Cook gently until soft. Divide between four ramekins.

Place the cream in a saucepan and heat until almost boiling. Place the egg yolks and sugar in a bowl and beat together until pale. Slowly pour over the hot cream, whisking all the time. Strain the mixture back into the pan and add the vanilla. Cook over a very gentle heat, stirring constantly, until the mixture has thickened to a thick custard.

Divide the custard between the ramekins and leave to cool. Once cool, refrigerate for 4 hours, or overnight if possible.

When ready to serve the brulees, remove from the fridge and dredge the tops of the ramekins with a thick layer of icing sugar. Blow torch the sugar or grill under a very hot grill, until dark, golden brown and caramelised. Serve immediately.

Shirley's free range hens enjoy a GM- and antibiotic-free diet, as well as fantastic views of Chatsworth park.

Shirley Buckingham,
Mistlehall Farm, Rowsley.

Individual Cinnamon Pavlovas
with Apples and Brambles

Whisk the egg whites until stiff, add a dash of lemon juice and then gradually whisk in the granulated sugar. Fold in the caster sugar, cornflour and cinnamon, the meringue should be thick and shiny. Shape the mixture into four individual pavlovas on the lined baking sheet and cook in the preheated oven for 45 - 50 minutes, until the pavlovas are dry and will lift easily from the paper.

Meanwhile, place the apples in a saucepan with the sugar, mixed spice and another dash of lemon juice. Cook over a gentle heat until softened. Add the brambles and leave to cool.

When the meringues are cool, top with the apple and bramble mixture and a spoonful of crème fraiche or yoghurt.

2 egg whites
1 lemon, juiced
55g granulated sugar
55g caster sugar
¼ tsp cornflour
½ tsp ground cinnamon
2 eating apples, peeled, cored and diced
30g caster sugar
½ tsp mixed spice
110g brambles
Crème fraiche or yoghurt, to serve

Preheat the oven to 130°C/250°F/Gas Mark ½

Line a baking sheet with non-stick baking parchment

Serves 4

Autumn

Chatsworth Raspberry Bakewell Tart

First make the pastry. Sift together the flour, salt and icing sugar. Rub in the cold butter using a food processor or your fingertips until the mixture resembles fine breadcrumbs. Mix the egg yolk with the cold water and add to the mixture to bring together. Shape the pastry into a flat disc and chill in the fridge for half an hour. Roll out the pastry and use to line a 23cm loose bottomed tart tin. Prick the base with a fork and chill for half an hour or until the pastry is solid.

Line the pastry case with a circle of greaseproof paper, fill with baking beans and bake blind for 15 minutes. Remove the beans and bake for a further 5 minutes until the pastry is dry and biscuity. Remove the pastry case from the oven and leave to cool. Turn the oven down to 190°C/375°F/Gas Mark 5.

When cool, spread the jam over the bottom of the pastry case and scatter over the raspberries. Whisk together the eggs, sugar, almond extract and vanilla seeds until pale. Add the melted butter and whisk until well combined. Finally fold in the ground almonds. Spoon this mixture over the raspberries and bake the tart for 20 minutes.

Sprinkle the flaked almonds over the top and bake for a further 10 minutes, until the filling is set and golden brown. Dust with icing sugar and serve warm, with cream or icecream.

For the pastry
175g plain flour
25g icing sugar
125g unsalted butter, chilled and diced
1 large egg yolk
2 tablespoons cold water

For the filling
3tbsp Chatsworth raspberry jam
200g raspberries
1 egg yolk
3 eggs
110g caster sugar
2 tsp almond extract
1 vanilla pod, halved and seeds removed
110g unsalted butter, melted
110g ground almonds
Handful flaked almonds

Serves 8

Preheat the oven to 200°C/400°F/Gas Mark 6

Autumn

Honey and Mascarpone Orange Cream
with Black Pepper Biscuits

1 tbsp powdered gelatine
125g mascarpone
1 vanilla pod, halved
and seeds removed
1 orange, zested and juiced
85g runny honey
30g caster sugar
500ml double cream

1 egg white
50g caster sugar
25g plain flour
¼ tsp black pepper,
freshly ground
25g unsalted butter, melted

Preheat the oven to
190°C/375°F/Gas Mark 5

Serves 4

Place 3 tablespoons of water in a small saucepan, sprinkle on the gelatine and leave to soak for 1 minute. Heat over a very gentle heat until the gelatine has dissolved.

Whisk together the mascarpone, vanilla seeds, orange zest, juice, honey and caster sugar. Add the dissolved gelatine and mix well. Whip the cream until it just holds its shape, then fold in to the mascarpone mixture. Spoon into four individual serving dishes and chill until set.

For the black pepper biscuits, whisk the egg white until frothy, then whisk in the sugar. Fold in the flour and black pepper and finally the melted butter. Line a baking sheet with non stick baking parchment or silicone paper. Drop teaspoons of the mixture onto the lined baking sheet and spread into thin rounds. Bake in the preheated oven for 4 - 5 minutes, until golden brown around the edges. Transfer to a wire rack to cool, or mould over a rolling pin, leave to set and remove.

Remove the creams from the fridge 10 minutes before you want to serve them. Serve on plates with the black pepper biscuits on the side.

puddings

Autumn

Winter

to start

Blinis with Smoked Eel, Bacon and Horseradish

First make the blinis. Sift the flour and baking powder into a bowl with a pinch of salt. Make a well in the centre and add the eggs. With a whisk or wooden spoon, mix gently, drawing in flour from the edges, to make a smooth batter. Add enough milk to make a thick batter, probably between 50ml and 100ml, but dependent on the size of your eggs.

Melt the butter in a large frying pan. Drop tablespoons of the batter into the hot pan and cook for 2 - 3 minutes on each side, until golden brown and cooked through, you may have to do this in batches. Keep the blinis warm in a low oven.

Pan fry or grill the bacon until crisp. Mix together the crème fraiche and horseradish sauce and season. To serve, place a couple of warm blinis on each plate. Spoon some horseradish crème fraiche on top and divide the smoked eel between the plates. Top each plate with a rasher of crisp streaky bacon and garnish with a sprig of dill.

600g smoked eel fillet
4 rashers thinly cut smoked streaky bacon
200g crème fraiche
1 tbsp horseradish sauce
Dill sprigs, to garnish

For the blinis
85g plain flour
1 tsp baking powder
2 eggs
Full fat milk
30g butter

Serves 4

Pea and Roasted Garlic Soup

Cut the heads of garlic in half horizontally and drizzle with the olive oil. Wrap in foil and place on a baking sheet. Roast the garlic for 40 minutes, until completely soft.

Melt the butter in a large saucepan and add the onions. Cover and cook over a gentle heat for 10 minutes, until they are soft and translucent. Add the frozen peas and stir so that the peas are coated in the butter and onion mixture.

Pour in the stock and bring to the boil. Turn down the heat and simmer for 5 minutes. Remove the garlic from the oven and, when cool enough to handle, squeeze the soft roasted garlic cloves into the pan.

Purée with a hand blender and season to taste with sea salt and black pepper. Serve the soup with a spoonful of crème fraiche, garnished with a few chopped chives.

4 heads garlic
2 tbsp olive oil
50g butter
2 onions, peeled and roughly chopped
1 kg frozen peas
1 litre vegetable stock

To serve
55g crème fraiche
1 tbsp chives, finely chopped

Serves 4

Preheat the oven to
180°C/350°F/Gas Mark 4

Pan-Fried Smoked Salmon
and Pancetta with Avocado and Spinach Salad

100g pancetta, cubed
2 tbsp olive oil
250g smoked salmon, sliced
2 tbsp wholegrain mustard
4 tbsp crème fraiche
1 tbsp honey
2 tbsp chopped dill
250g baby spinach leaves
12 cherry tomatoes, halved
1 large avocado, stoned,
peeled and sliced
Brown bread and lemon
wedges, to serve

Serves 4

Heat half the oil in a non stick pan and fry the pancetta until crisp. Season the smoked salmon with black pepper and add to the pan. Fry for 1 minute then remove from the heat.

Mix together the mustard, crème fraiche, honey and dill and season to taste. Toss the spinach leaves in the remaining olive oil and divide between four plates with the tomatoes and avocado. Top with the smoked salmon and pancetta and drizzle over the mustard cream. Serve immediately, with fresh brown bread and lemon wedges.

Derbyshire Smokery use a variety of woods for smoking including oak, alder, mesquite and hickory, to match the distinct tastes of the meat and to offer something different.

Alan Hobson and Ian Jennings, Derbyshire Smokery, Flagg.

Balsamic Shallots with Derbyshire Prosciutto and Shavings of Lincolnshire Poacher

Heat the olive oil in a heavy bottomed pan and add the shallots. Cover and cook over a gentle heat for 10 minutes, until the shallots are starting to soften. Add the brown sugar and season with sea salt and black pepper. Cover and cook the shallots, stirring occasionally, for 30 minutes.

Add the vinegar and increase the heat. Cook until the liquid has evaporated and the shallots are sticky, glazed and caramelised. Remove from the heat and leave to cool. Once cool, tear in the basil leaves. Using a potato peeler, peel shavings of the Lincolnshire Poacher cheese.

To serve, divide the shallots and prosciutto between 4 plates. Scatter with the shavings of Lincolnshire Poacher and serve with some warm, crusty bread.

**20 shallots,
peeled and left whole
2 tbsp olive oil
2 tsp brown sugar
4 tbsp balsamic vinegar
Small bunch basil
125g sliced Derbyshire
prosciutto
60g Lincolnshire Poacher
cheese**

Serves 4

Caramelised Pear and Chicory Salad
with Stilton and a Sherry Vinaigrette

Mix together all the ingredients for the dressing, adding sea salt and black pepper to taste.

Cut the ends off the chicory and separate into individual leaves. In a saucepan heat the balsamic vinegar with the brown sugar for 30 seconds. Add the pears and cook for a further 3 - 4 minutes until the pears have softened and are coated in the balsamic syrup. Set aside and leave to cool.

Meanwhile grill the pancetta until brown and crispy. Leave to cool and break into pieces. Layer the chicory, watercress, crumbled Stilton and pears in a serving dish or salad bowl. Top with the pieces of pancetta and the walnuts and serve.

4 heads red chicory
2 tbsp balsamic vinegar
2 tsp brown sugar
2 pears, peeled,
cored and cut into eight
8 slices pancetta
1 bunch watercress,
trimmed and washed
200g Stilton, crumbled
55g walnuts, toasted

For the dressing
5 tbsp extra virgin olive oil
3 tbsp sherry vinegar
2 tbsp runny honey
1 tsp grain mustard
1 tsp Dijon mustard

Serves 4

Winter

main courses

Fillet of Venison
with Juniper Sauce, Parsnip Purée and Rösti Potatoes

First make the juniper sauce. Place the red wine and stock in a saucepan with the juniper berries and reduce by half. Season to taste and set aside.

For the parsnip purée, place the parsnips in a large bowl, add the olive oil, thyme, honey and lemon juice and season well. Mix together so that the parsnips are coated in the mixture, then tip onto a baking sheet. Roast in the preheated oven for 30 minutes until softened. Place in a food processor with the butter and process to a thick purée. Keep warm.

For the rösti potatoes, grate the potatoes onto a clean tea towel, sprinkle with salt and squeeze out any excess liquid. Place in a bowl and add the paprika and black pepper. Heat the oil in a frying pan. Spoon some of the potato mixture into an oiled metal cooking ring and pack down well. Remove the ring and repeat the process three more times. Cook the rösti for 5 minutes on each side, until well coloured, then transfer to a non stick baking sheet and finish in the oven for 5 - 10 minutes, or until cooked through.

To serve the venison, heat the butter with the oil in a frying pan. Pat the meat dry and season with sea salt and black pepper. Pan fry the steaks for 2 minutes on each side, then remove from the pan and rest for a few minutes. Whisk the butter and double cream into the juniper sauce. Place the rösti on a warmed plate, top with the venison and spoon some parsnip purée at the side. Spoon over the juniper sauce and serve.

4 x 200g
venison fillet steaks
20g butter
1 tbsp olive oil

For the juniper sauce
100ml red wine
150ml strong beef
or game stock
2 tbsp juniper berries
30g unsalted butter,
diced and chilled
30ml double cream

For the parsnip purée
500g parsnips, peeled and
cut into large dice
1 tbsp olive oil
sprig of thyme
½ tbsp honey
1 tbsp lemon juice
30g butter

For the rösti potatoes
2 large baking potatoes,
peeled
2 tsp paprika
2 tbsp vegetable oil

Serves 4

Preheat the oven to
180°C/350°F/Gas Mark 4

Spiced Beef
with Beetroot, Shallots and Crème Fraiche

Melt the butter with the olive oil in a heavy bottomed casserole. Brown the beef in batches over a high heat. Remove from the pan and set aside.

Reduce the heat and add the shallots to the pan. Cook for 5 - 10 minutes until lightly golden, then add the garlic and cook for a further minute. Stir in the brown sugar, allspice and juniper berries and cook for a few minutes, until the sugar caramelises the shallots, then add the flour and cook out for 1 minute. Add the red wine and balsamic vinegar, then blend in the stock. Return the beef to the pan and add the beetroot. Cover and cook in the preheated oven for 1½ - 2 hours until the beef is tender.

Remove the casserole from the oven and skim off the fat if there is any. Mix together the crème fraiche, mustard and horseradish and stir into the casserole before serving.

1kg stewing beef or skirt, cut into 3cm cubes
20g butter
2 tbsp olive oil
16 whole shallots, peeled
2 cloves garlic, peeled and crushed
1 tbsp brown sugar
2 tsp ground allspice
8 juniper berries, crushed
2 tbsp plain flour
290ml red wine
1 tbsp balsamic vinegar
290ml beef stock
8 small beetroots, peeled and halved
2 tbsp crème fraiche
2 tbsp dry mustard
3 tbsp creamed horseradish

Serves 4

Preheat the oven to
150°C/300°F/Gas Mark 2

Winter

Carrots with Grainy Mustard and Maple Syrup

**500g carrots, peeled and
quartered lengthways
2 tbsp olive oil
2 tbsp whole grain mustard
3 tbsp maple syrup**

Preheat the oven to
220°C/425°F/Gas Mark 7

Serves 4, as a side dish

Bring a large pan of salted water to the boil and add the
carrots. Cook for 2 - 3 minutes, then drain well.

Place the carrots in a roasting tin and drizzle over the olive oil.
Season and roast in the preheated oven for 10 - 15 minutes,
until just starting to brown.

Mix together the whole grain mustard and maple syrup and
pour over the carrots. Toss well, so that the carrots are coated
in the mixture and return to the oven for a further 5 - 10
minutes, until the carrots are sticky and caramelised. Serve
immediately.

Three generations of vegetable
growers work at Woodhouse Farm,
drilling and bunching carrots in
batches from March onwards to
ensure that customers get them at
their best.

Brian Heath, Woodhouse Farm,
Melbourne, Derbyshire.

Braised Lamb Shanks
with Mint and Harissa

Heat the oil in a large ovenproof casserole. Season the lamb shanks and brown well all over. Remove from the pan and set aside. Add the shallots and cook for 5 - 10 minutes until they are golden brown.

Reduce the heat and add the garlic, harissa, cumin seeds, paprika and allspice. Fry for 2 - 3 minutes, then add the plum tomatoes and stock. Stir in half of the mint and coriander and return the lamb shanks to the pan.

Cover the pan and braise the lamb shanks in the preheated oven for 2 - 2½ hours, until they are tender and the meat is falling away from the bone. Remove the lamb shanks from the casserole and keep warm. Bring the cooking liquor to the boil and reduce until it has thickened slightly. Adjust the seasoning to taste and return the lamb to the pan. Sprinkle over the remaining mint and coriander and serve.

4 lamb shanks
2 tbsp olive oil
16 shallots, peeled
2 cloves garlic,
peeled and crushed
1 tbsp harissa paste
2 tsp cumin seeds
2 tsp paprika
2 tsp allspice
2 tins plum tomatoes
550ml good lamb or
chicken stock
½ bunch mint,
roughly chopped
½ bunch coriander,
roughly chopped

Serves 4

Preheat the oven to
170°C/325°F/Gas Mark 3

Breast of Pheasant
with Orange, Cardamom and Creamed Cabbage

4 pheasant supremes,
with skin on
30g butter
50ml olive oil
4 tsp cardamom pods
2 oranges, juiced
150ml Madeira
125ml game stock
30g unsalted butter,
diced and chilled

For the creamed cabbage
1 Savoy cabbage,
finely shredded
30g butter
50g pine nuts
1 clove garlic,
peeled and finely chopped
freshly grated nutmeg
50ml double cream

Preheat the oven to
180°C/350°F/Gas Mark 4

First prepare the creamed cabbage. Melt the butter in a large frying pan or wok, add the cabbage and stir fry for 2 - 3 minutes. Add the pine nuts and garlic and cook for a further 2 minutes, stirring constantly, then add the cream and season with sea salt, black pepper and the nutmeg. Reduce until the cream has thickened and set aside.

Season the pheasant breasts with sea salt and black pepper. Heat an ovenproof sauté pan, melt the butter with the oil and sear the breasts on both sides. Sprinkle the cardamom pods into the pan followed by the juice of one orange and half the Madeira.

Cover and roast in the preheated oven for 8 - 10 minutes until the pheasant is pink. Remove the pheasant and set it aside to rest. Deglaze the pan with the remaining madeira, then add the remaining orange juice and the game stock. Bring to the boil and reduce for 5 minutes, then sieve the sauce into a clean saucepan and whisk in the cold, diced butter.

Carve the pheasant and serve with the creamed cabbage, with the sauce spooned over.

Set up by Barry Hodgkinson, the South Derbyshire Growers deliver baskets of fresh produce to Chatsworth farm shop throughout the year.

Martin Sharp and Barry Hodgkinson, South Derbyshire Growers

Quick Sausage Casserole
with Roasted Garlic Mash

Cut the head of garlic in half horizontally and drizzle the cut sides with a little oil. Wrap the garlic in foil and place on a baking sheet. Roast in the preheated oven for 40 minutes, until the garlic is soft. Place the potatoes in a large pan of salted water and bring to the boil. Simmer until tender, drain well and mash or purée through a ricer. Season with sea salt and black pepper and squeeze in the roasted garlic cloves. Beat in the remaining rapeseed oil and keep warm.

Heat the vegetable oil in a large, heavy based casserole pan and brown off the sausages on all sides. Remove from the pan and set aside. Add the olive oil to the pan, followed by the red onion. Cover and cook for 5 - 10 minutes, until softened. Remove the lid and add the garlic and mushrooms. Cook for a further 5 minutes. Stir in the tomato purée, balsamic vinegar, redcurrant jelly, thyme and bay leaf, then blend in the red wine. Return the sausages to the pan and add the lentils. Simmer gently for 15 minutes, until the sausages are cooked through and serve with the roasted garlic mash.

8 good quality pork sausages
1 tbsp vegetable oil
3 tbsp olive oil
1 large red onion, peeled and finely sliced
2 garlic cloves, peeled and crushed
110g button mushrooms
1 tsp tomato purée
1 tbsp balsamic vinegar
1 tbsp redcurrant jelly
1 sprig thyme
1 bay leaf
2 glasses red wine
200g tinned green lentils

For the mash
1 kg floury potatoes, peeled and cut into large dice
1 head garlic
4 tbsp rapeseed oil

Serves 4

Preheat the oven to
180°C/350°F/Gas Mark 4

Winter

Honeyed Duck
with Pea and Potato Mash and Red Wine Sauce

Heat half the butter in a heavy-based saucepan and add the shallots. Cook for 10 minutes over a medium heat, stirring from time to time, until golden brown. Deglaze the pan with the red wine, then add the stock, sugar and thyme. Reduce for 10 minutes, then add the cranberries. Reduce the heat and cook for a further 10 - 15 minutes, until there is a glossy liquid coating the shallots and cranberries and the shallots are tender. Remove from the heat and keep warm.

Place the potatoes, cut into medium-sized pieces, into a pan of salted water, bring to the boil and cook for 15 - 20 minutes or until nearly tender. Add the peas, return to the boil and simmer for a further minute. Drain in a colander, return the pan to the heat, melt the remaining butter and add the double cream and the nutmeg. Then add the peas and potatoes back to the pan and mash well. Adjust the seasoning to taste and keep warm.

Score the skin of the duck breasts in a criss-cross pattern. Season with sea salt and black pepper and place, skin side down, in a frying pan. Cook until the skin begins to crisp. Turn and seal the duck breasts on the meat side for a further minute. Remove them from the pan, place in a small roasting tin and brush with the honey. Cook in the top half of the oven for 10 - 15 minutes for pink, or 20 minutes for medium, basting with the honey mixture as necessary.

Remove the duck from the oven and rest for a couple of minutes. Place a spoonful of mashed potato on a warm plate, slice the duck breast into three or four pieces and place on top of the mash. Arrange three or four shallots at the side of the duck breast and drizzle with the red wine sauce.

4 duck breasts
1 tbsp runny honey

For the red wine sauce
12 shallots, peeled
250ml red wine
200ml chicken stock
2 tsp caster sugar
1 sprig thyme
55g fresh cranberries

For the mash
600g potatoes, peeled
300g frozen peas
100g butter, melted
2 tbsp double cream
Pinch nutmeg

Serves 4

Preheat the oven to
200°C/400°F/Gas Mark 6

Roast Rib of Chatsworth Beef
with Mustard and Thyme Yorkshire Puddings

**5kg joint of
Chatsworth beef
2 tbsp olive oil
30g soft butter
2 tbsp plain flour
120ml red wine
1 litre good beef stock**

For the Yorkshire puddings
**2 tbsp rapeseed oil
110g plain flour
½ tsp baking powder
2 eggs, lightly beaten
100ml milk
50ml cold water
1 tbsp fresh thyme leaves
½ tbsp wholegrain mustard**

Serves 10

Pre-heat the oven to
220ºC/425ºF/Gas Mark 7

Rub the beef with the olive oil and soft butter and lightly season with sea salt. Place the joint in a sturdy roasting tin and roast in the hot oven for 30 minutes until the meat is well browned and sizzling. Turn the oven down to 170˚C/325º/Gas Mark 3 then cook for 12 - 15 mins per 500g for rare or 18/20 mins per 500g for well done.

Remove the meat from the oven and transfer to a warm plate. Loosely cover with a piece of foil and leave to rest for at least 30 mins before carving.

Meanwhile, make the Yorkshire puddings. Heat the oven to 220˚C/425º F/Gas Mark 7. Place a little oil into each section of a muffin tin and heat in the oven for 2 minutes.

Sift the flour and baking powder into a bowl. Make a well in the centre of the flour and add the beaten egg. Draw the flour into the egg, then gradually whisk in the milk and water until you have a smooth batter. Add the mustard and thyme leaves, season well. Transfer the mixture to a jug and pour into the hot muffin tin, filling each section ⅓ full. Place in the oven and bake for 20 - 25 mins without opening the oven door.

To make the gravy, add the flour to the meat juices and blend well. Add the red wine and bring to the boil, then blend in the stock. Simmer for 5 - 10 mins and season well. Sieve and serve with the beef, Yorkshire puddings and good quality creamed horseradish.

Game Casserole
with Port and Wild Mushrooms

Place the wild mushrooms in a bowl and cover with boiling water. Leave to soak for 30 minutes.

Heat the oil in a large, heavy based casserole. Add the pheasant and partridge joints and brown well on all sides. Remove from the pan and reserve. Add the bacon, shallots, onion and carrot and cook for 5 - 10 minutes until lightly browned. Stir in the garlic and cook for a further minute.

Add the soaked mushrooms to the pan, then sprinkle in the flour, stirring well. Add the tomato purée and tomatoes, then blend in the port, red wine and stock. Bring to the boil, turn down to a simmer and add the Cumberland sauce, thyme, bay leaf and juniper berries. Return the pheasant and partridge to the pan, cover and cook in the preheated oven for 45 minutes to an hour, until the meat is tender. Adjust the seasoning and serve.

1 pheasant, jointed
2 partridges, jointed
3 tbsp olive oil
150g smoked streaky bacon, finely chopped
12 shallots
1 onion,
peeled and finely chopped
1 carrot,
peeled and finely chopped
2 cloves garlic,
peeled and crushed
30g dried wild mushrooms
2 tbsp plain flour
2 tbsp tomato purée
4 tomatoes,
peeled, deseeded and finely chopped
150ml port
150ml red wine
500ml game stock
1 tbsp Cumberland sauce
2 sprigs thyme
1 bay leaf
10 juniper berries

Serves 4

Preheat the oven to
170°C/325°F/Gas Mark 3

Ian Turner, Farms Manager at Chatsworth, is responsible for all farming activities on the in-hand farms. Cattle raised for beef at Chatsworth include pure-bred and cross-bred Limousin.

Ian Turner, Farms Manager, Chatsworth

Roasted Shallots
with Apples and Cranberries

Place the shallots in a roasting tin and sprinkle over the olive oil, sugar, balsamic vinegar and cinnamon. Season with sea salt and black pepper and toss together so that the shallots are well coated. Roast in the preheated oven for 20 minutes.

Add the apple pieces, stir well and return to the oven for a further 10 - 15 minutes, until the shallots and apples are golden, sticky and caramelised. Scatter over the cranberries and return to the oven to heat through.

Serve as an accompaniment to pork chops, or as a side dish for Christmas.

500g shallots,
peeled and left whole
2 tbsp olive oil
½ tbsp soft light
brown sugar
1 tbsp balsamic vinegar
1 tsp cinnamon
2 eating apples,
peeled, cored and cut
into large pieces
75g dried cranberries

Serves 4, as a side dish

Preheat the oven to
190ºC/375ºF/Gas Mark 5

Winter

puddings

Pannetone, Chatsworth Marmalade and Whisky Bread and Butter Pudding

Butter an ovenproof dish. Thickly slice the pannetone and spread with the softened butter, followed by the marmalade. Arrange the slices in the buttered dish.

Whisk together the eggs, cream, milk, sugar, vanilla extract and whisky and pour over the pannetone, pressing it down so that it soaks up the custard. Place the dish in a roasting tin and pour in a couple of inches of hot water, so that it comes half way up the sides of the dish. Place carefully in the oven and bake for 35 - 40 minutes, until just set.

Dust with icing sugar and serve with double cream.

500g pannetone
50g unsalted butter, softened
1 jar Chatsworth Marmalade and Whisky Preserve, or other marmalade
6 eggs, beaten
425ml double cream
150ml full fat milk
75g caster sugar
½ tsp vanilla extract
1 tbsp whisky

Serves 6 - 8

Preheat the oven to
170°C/325°F/Gas Mark 3

Carrot Christmas Pudding

Grease a 1 litre pudding basin. Take a saucepan large enough to hold the pudding basin, fill with 7cm of water and bring to the boil.

In a large bowl, mix together the breadcrumbs, currants, raisins, suet, mixed peel, caster sugar, carrots and nutmeg. Make a well in the centre and add the beaten eggs, brandy and half of the milk. Mix together well and add the remaining milk as necessary to make a spoonable mixture of a dropping consistency.

Pour into the greased pudding basin and cover with a double layer of greaseproof paper, followed by a layer of foil. Tie securely with string and place in the saucepan, making sure that the water does not touch the foil.

Cover and steam for 3 hours, checking regularly and topping up with extra water as necessary. Turn out the pudding, dust with icing sugar and serve with custard, brandy butter or double cream.

300g fresh white breadcrumbs
225g currants
225g raisins
225g suet
55g mixed peel
225g caster sugar
2 large carrots, grated
¼ nutmeg, grated
2 large eggs, beaten
75ml brandy
150ml full-fat milk

Serves 6 - 8

Black Cherry, Almond and Chocolate Strudel

1 tin pitted black cherries, drained and coarsely chopped
1 tbsp kirsch
100g whole blanched almonds, lightly toasted
250g good quality plain chocolate
50g ground almonds
5 tbsp caster sugar
1 box filo pastry
125g unsalted butter, melted
Icing sugar, to serve

Serves 8

Preheat the oven to 180°C/350°F/Gas Mark 4

Soak the cherries in the kirsch and set aside. Place the whole almonds, chocolate and 2 tbsp of the sugar into a food processor and pulse until coarsely chopped. Cover the pastry with a damp tea towel to prevent it from drying out. Mix the remaining sugar with the ground almonds.

Lay out a sheet of pastry and brush with melted butter. Place a second sheet on top, brush with more melted butter then sprinkle over a third of the almond and sugar mixture. Cover with a third sheet of pastry, brush with melted butter and sprinkle over the second third of the remaining almond and sugar mixture. Top with a fourth sheet of pastry, brush with butter and sprinkle with the remaining mixture. Top with a final sheet and brush with butter.

Spread the chocolate mixture on top of the pastry leaving a 4cm border. Spread the cherries over the centre and tuck in the edges. Firmly roll into a log, place seamside down on a greased baking sheet and brush with the remaining butter.

Bake in the preheated oven for 30 - 35 mins until golden brown. Cool slightly on a wire rack before dusting with icing sugar and serving with cream.

puddings

Amaretti Roulade
with Mascarpone and Festive Fruits

For the filling, place all the dried fruit in a bowl and pour over the Madeira. Leave to soak for 30 minutes.

Bring a pan of water to the boil. Place the eggs, sugar and almond essence in a bowl, remove the pan from the heat and set the bowl over it. Whisk the eggs and sugar over the heat until they form a thick, pale foam. Sift over the flour and sprinkle in the Amaretti biscuit crumbs and fold in. Pour the mixture into the lined Swiss roll tin and bake for 10 minutes, until risen and light golden brown. Leave to cool in the tin.

Beat together the double cream and mascarpone until thick. Fold in the vanilla essence and amaretto liqueur.

Lay out a piece of greaseproof paper larger than the Swiss roll tin and dust it heavily with icing sugar. Turn the roulade out onto it, browned side down. Cover with the cream and mascarpone mixture and lay the soaked fruits down the middle. Roll the roulade firmly into a log and chill, wrapped in the paper and sitting on its seam, for 2 hours.

To serve, carefully unwrap the roulade and place on a serving platter. Dust with some more icing sugar and serve.

100g Amaretti biscuits, crushed
3 large eggs
110g caster sugar
1 tsp almond essence
40g self-raising flour

For the filling
400ml double cream
250g mascarpone cheese
1 tsp vanilla essence
2 tbsp amaretto liqueur
55g dried figs, sliced
55g dried dates, sliced
30g prunes, sliced
30g dried cranberries
30g sultanas
3 tbsp Madeira
Icing sugar

Serves 6 - 8

Preheat the oven to
200°C/400°F/Gas Mark 6

Line a Swiss roll tin with
baking parchment

Port and Blackberry Jelly
with Mulled Fruits

4 sheets leaf gelatine
450g blackberries
200g caster sugar
30ml cassis
150ml port
150ml red grape juice

For the mulled fruits
250ml red wine
120g caster sugar
1 cinnamon stick
4 star anise
2 strips orange zest
6 dried figs
12 prunes
12 dried apricots
85g dried cranberries

Serves 4

Place the gelatine sheets in a shallow bowl, cover with cold water and leave to soften. Place the blackberries and caster sugar in a saucepan, cover with 150ml water and bring to the boil. Simmer for 2 - 3 minutes, then remove from the heat and add the cassis and port.

In another pan, heat the red grape juice. Drain the softened gelatine, add to the warm grape juice and heat gently until the gelatine has dissolved. Add this to the blackberry mixture. Rinse four ramekins with cold water, then pour in the jelly mixture and refrigerate for 4 hours, or overnight.

For the mulled fruits, place the red wine and caster sugar in a saucepan and heat gently until the sugar has dissolved. Add the cinnamon stick, star anise, orange zest and dried fruit and simmer for 5 minutes. Remove from the heat and pour into a bowl. Leave to cool and infuse for at least 2 hours.

Turn the jellies out onto plates and place some of the mulled fruits at the side. Serve with clotted cream.

puddings

Winter

Index

Metric Conversion Scales

Oven temperature scales

°C	°F	Gas Mark
110°C	225°F	¼
130	250	½
140	275	1
150	300	2
170	325	3
180	350	4
190	375	5
200	400	6
220	425	7
230	450	8
240	475	9

Weight conversions

Grams	Ounces
30g	1oz
55g	2oz
85g	3oz
110g	4oz
150g	5oz
180g	6oz
200g	7oz
225g	8oz
250g	9oz
275g	10oz
315g	11oz
350g	12oz
375g	13oz
400g	14oz

1kg is equal to 2.2lb

Liquid conversions

Metric	Imperial	Fl oz
5ml	1 tsp	
15ml	1 tbsp	
25ml		1fl oz
75ml	4 tbsp	3fl oz
100ml		4fl oz
150ml	¼ pt	5fl oz
290ml	½ pt	10fl oz
290ml	½ pt	10fl oz
575ml	1 pt	20fl oz
700ml	1 ¼ pt	25fl oz
850ml	1 ½ pt	30fl oz
1l	1 ¾ pt	35 fl oz